'It's almost 50 years since the Equal Pay Act, women are doing brilliantly in education — and yet gender, and gender inequalities, are still huge issues. *The Paula Principle* tells us both why and why we should care. It's a splendid analysis, a fascinating read — and a great way to understand just how differently women, as well as men, experience today's reality.'
Alison Wolf, Professor the Baroness Wolf of Dulwich

'Essential reading for anyone who thinks about the future of work — compelling evidence showing how unions help women and men build alternative working lives, and a powerful argument for radical changes to achieve genuine equality.'
Frances O'Grady, General Secretary of the Trades Union Congress

'Why do women tend to outperform men in education, yet earn less in the labour market? A society where women work below their level of competence is missing out on the chance to reach its potential. Tom Schuller shows that gender inequity should concern all of us.'
Andrew Leigh MP, author of *The Economics of Just About Everything*

'In a world where women's work, despite changes in the last decades, is still given less recognition than men's at every level, and where the gap is closing slowly if at all, it lifts the spirits to find Tom Schuller's thoughtful book analysing with subtlety and elegance why this might be so.'
Ursula Owen, founder-director of Virago Press

The Paula Principle

Tom Schuller has worked in adult education most of his life, as a teacher, researcher, international bureaucrat, and policy analyst. His posts have included Dean of the Faculty of Continuing Education at Birkbeck, University of London; Head of the Centre for Educational Research and Innovation at OECD in Paris; and Professor of Lifelong Learning at the University of Edinburgh. His previous books have covered a range of topics, from the benefits of lifelong learning to industrial democracy and social capital. He lives in London and struggles to learn the clarinet, and to play semi-competent tennis.

For Bernie, Jo-Anna, and Prue, with love

the
Paula
Principle⚥

why women lose out at work — and what needs to be done about it

Tom Schuller

SCRIBE

Melbourne • London

Scribe Publications
2 John St, Clerkenwell, London, WC1N 2ES, United Kingdom
18–20 Edward St, Brunswick, Victoria 3056, Australia

First published by Scribe 2017
This edition published 2018

Copyright © Tom Schuller 2017

Typeset in Minion Pro 11.75/17.25pt by the publishers
Printed and bound in the UK by CIP Group (UK) Ltd, Croydon CR0 4YY

Drawings by Cloe Floirat

Scribe Publications is committed to the sustainable use of natural resources and
the use of paper products made responsibly from those resources.

9781911344605 (UK edition)
9781925321982 (Australian edition)
9781925548013 (e-book)

CiP data records for this title are available from the National Library of
Australia and the British Library.

scribepublications.co.uk
scribepublications.com.au

Contents

Preface

The notion of a Paula Principle first cropped up when I was conducting research for a rather prosaic paper on skills and equality for the UK Commission for Employment and Skills. I've worked most of my life in educational organisations of different kinds, so I'd long known that girls outperform boys academically, and that there are more women than men in colleges and universities. I also knew from first-hand experience that women are generally keener than men to take part in most forms of adult education. But I was genuinely surprised to discover that, in the United Kingdom at least, women also participate more than men in training in the workplace, boosting their vocational skills.

I had always thought that women's disadvantages at work included less access to this kind of professional development. So did the Commission for Employment and Skills — that's why they asked me to write the paper, as one of a series on disadvantaged groups. Now I found that they go on learning more than men in this sphere, as in almost every other. So the 'competence gap' between women and men is one that is growing fast, on almost every dimension.

This meant that I had to give the Commission for Employment and Skills paper an entirely different slant than I had been planning. Women may not experience inequality in access to skills, but once the picture is extended to include what happens as a result of the learning, it reveals a far wider and highly intriguing issue. Why does women's lifelong accumulation of competences not seem to have had the impact that we might expect on careers and rewards at work?

Sociologists, labour economists, and many others have analysed exhaustively why women don't get certain types of job or progress beyond certain levels, and why gender pay gaps exist. Many of the specific issues raised in this book have already been identified and investigated in far greater depth than I can hope to do. But the way the competence gap between women and men is increasing, in almost every developed country, gives added salience to the question of how and why women's competences are not recognised and rewarded as men's are. That competence gap is increasing faster than the gap between the pay and career patterns of men and women is closing. What jumped into my head — and ultimately prompted me to write the book — was the mirror-image symmetry between this notion of women's competence and the famous (or once-famous) Peter Principle, that 'every employee rises to his [sic] level of incompetence'. The mirror image is the Paula Principle: 'Most women work below their level of competence.'

This simple contrast, between the relative competence levels of the two sexes and their rewards at work, seemed to strike an instant chord with almost anyone I mentioned it to. The notion of a Paula Principle elicited such immediate, energetic, and quite varied responses that it looked like a useful trigger for further debate. I'm not a gender specialist, and have no especial authority on gender issues. This book is intended simply to give long-running debates some fresh angles: on how we might shift the discussion about 'equality' forwards, beyond looking for identical outcomes for women and men; on what we mean by the term 'career'; and on how we might do better so that what people earn really reflects their value. The debate will take very different forms in different contexts: it applies variously to bank workers in London and to care workers in Melbourne, to employees in a US multinational and to the staff of a small company in Brazil, and so on.

In particular, although I'm a true believer in the value and power of education, I'm disturbed by how much emphasis is placed on education alone as the solution to problems that are much broader and that call into question the way work is organised and its rewards distributed. The Paula Principle demonstrates this clearly: enabling women to acquire yet more education and training will not solve the social and economic issues that define the gender debate. Pious proclamations on the value of learning are all very well, but we need now to look much more closely at the result of this learning — and what determines these results.

I do not for one moment hold the view that education is only or even primarily about getting higher salaries or bigger jobs. For men and women, education is and should be about personal development, informed citizenship, curiosity, tolerance, positive mental and physical health, cultural creativity, and much more. The Paula Principle does not apply to these things, because the rewards in these areas are as great for women as they are for men. It is in the sphere of the workplace that the Paula Principle finds its application. But this means much more than disparity in wages and salaries. It includes non-material factors such as the fulfilment of aspirations, job satisfaction, and, crucially, the realisation of potential. These are major rewards, even if we cannot put a financial price on them.

So this is my hope: that writing about the Paula Principle will help us to think through how and why people are rewarded — in this broad sense — for the work they do, and then to act if we think that the reward systems could and should be better.

As a man writing primarily about what is and isn't happening to women at work, I've at times struggled to find an appropriate voice.[1] Very obviously I can't speak with the kind of subjective experience that might give a richer tone. I interviewed about 40 women (and a few men), recruited unscientifically, from a variety of backgrounds and with various occupational histories. I hope it's clear that I don't think I speak for women. I can't even claim particular direct exposure to the issues raised. My mother's career started after she'd raised her children to semi-independence; it culminated as the head teacher of a small school, and more than satisfied her. I have two daughters, which has maybe subconsciously sensitised me to some of the issues, but confers no authority (far from it). I've been a manager with talented female staff, but have not been directly confronted by gender issues in any major way, at least not knowingly. Yet I do care strongly about fairness; about treating complex issues with respect and curiosity; and about contributing to a better public debate.

I have tried to be alert to the issues of language and syntax, as well. Sometimes I can use 'we' and 'our' quite comfortably — when I say, for example, that better part-time careers will enable our skills to be used to full effect, this means in the social and family spheres as well as at work, and by men as well as women. There are other times when 'we' cannot work, where it would not make any sense for me to bracket myself in with the women I'm talking about or talking to; but at the same time 'they' would sound curiously distant, and would almost imply that I'm writing for men about women. I have dealt with all this as best I can. My intention has been to include everyone in the conversation. Indeed, my main conclusion — that women will only get to use their competences fully under a different workplace regime — addresses an issue that concerns men as much as women. Maybe the fact that a man is saying so will give the debate some added impetus.

1

The Principle Twins

Paula and Peter

'Every employee tends to rise to his level of incompetence.'
The Peter Principle

'Most women work below their level of competence.'
The Paula Principle

George Eliot gives us a natural starting point for our discussion about how women's skills and talents are undervalued. She was, after all, the 19th-century female author who had to write under a man's name in order to increase her chances of being taken seriously. Maggie Tulliver is the feisty heroine in Eliot's novel *The Mill on the Floss*. She has a brother, Tom. Maggie's father, a comfortably off but uneducated miller, is a kindly man who wants the best for his children, and in one memorable scene he debates with his wife, Bessy, how to go about this. He is keen for Tom to have 'a good eddication ... I should like Tom to be a bit of a scholard, so as he might be up to the tricks o' these fellows as talk fine and write with a flourish.'[1] He has in mind a career for Tom as 'a sort of engineer', or a surveyor, or an auctioneer. The trouble is that Tom is not exactly a star learner. Even Mr Tulliver recognises that he's 'a bit slowish', telling Bessy that Tom takes after her side of the family. Amiable Bessy accepts this without protest; after all, Tom does like a lot of salt in his broth, just like her brother and her father before him.

They agree that the brains from their union have gone to Tom's little sister, Maggie. 'The little un takes after my side, now,' says Mr Tulliver. 'She's twice as 'cute as Tom. Too 'cute for a woman, I'm afraid. It's no mischief much while she's a little un, but an over-'cute woman's no better nor a long-tailed sheep — she'll fetch none the bigger price for that.'[2] Mr Tulliver is genuinely proud of his daughter's acuteness. He tells his good friend Mr Riley that she can read 'straight off, as if she knowed it all beforehand. And allays at her book!' Then he checks himself: 'But it's bad — it's bad … a woman's no business wi' being so clever; it'll turn to trouble, I doubt.'

Maggie never gets the education at which she might have excelled, while Tom goes to an academy but struggles to learn even basic skills. He is a decent lad, but he has a hard time maintaining his superiority over his clever younger sister. There is, though, one area where he will always be the winner. When Maggie offers him some money to make up for the fact that his pet rabbit died while in her care, he exclaims, 'I don't want *your* money, you silly thing. I've got a great deal more money than you, because I'm a boy. I always have half-sovereigns and sovereigns for my Christmas boxes, because I shall be a man, and you only have five-shilling pieces, because you're only a girl.'[3]

Much has changed in our expectations of girls and boys since George Eliot so memorably sketched the Tullivers and their different destinies. Some things have changed faster than others, and it's exactly the contrasting differences in the pace and scale of change that have prompted this book. We now applaud and encourage acuteness in girls, or at least its modern equivalent: educational achievement. We expect women to succeed at school and college, and they do so, in far greater numbers than men. But when it comes to the material returns to education, change has been a lot slower. This is even though women's learning routinely outstrips men's by nearly as much as Maggie outsmarted her brother. Progress towards equality in the way we reward competence has slowed to a crawl or even stalled. Women's earnings might not be stuck at five shillings to the men's sovereign (that is, at 25% in the currency of the time), but they have not caught up, let alone passed, those of men. The issue is emphatically not only about money: women's work is given less recognition at every level, and women's careers have a lower and flatter trajectory. In short, we have on the one side a widening *female/male competence gap*, and on the other a *male/female gap in the rewards that work brings*, which is closing only slowly, if at all. It is this contrast that generates the Paula Principle.

Fast-forward 70 years and move north from the Tullivers' imaginary Lincolnshire home to Yorkshire in the 1930s. In Winifred Holtby's *South Riding*, published in 1936, Lydia Holly is, on the face of it, not at all like Maggie Tulliver. Her circumstances are not the relatively comfortable ones of an established miller with just two children to raise. She is much lower down the social and economic scale, as the eldest daughter of a large and poor family living in a converted railway carriage. She lacks Maggie's personal charm; she is 'an untidy fat loutish girl in a torn overall'.[4] But, like Maggie, she shows evident signs of cleverness.

Unlike Maggie's mother, Lydia's mother identifies and values her daughter's potential, and does her best to give her a chance to develop it. Lydia had been deprived of taking up the place she had won at the high school at the age of 11 because she was needed to escort her younger sisters to the village school. But her mother, being a fighter, insists Lydia gets a second chance when Daisy, her youngest sister, is old enough. Lydia takes it, with gusto. Alas, her mother dies in yet another childbirth, and so Lydia is taken out of school to help run the family home. The young and idealistic headmistress of the school,

Sarah Burton, plans her rescue. But by now 'Lydia believed in promises no longer … At 16 a forlorn cynicism quenched her once robust vitality … She knew that she was clever. But something had broken in her spirit.'[5] Although she is eventually able to return to school, as far as readers can tell she never fulfils any of her early promise.

By the 1930s, when *South Riding* was written, parents' attitudes towards the education of their daughters had changed a lot since the Tullivers' day.[6] They no longer assumed that the most a girl could want from an education was a set of social skills to equip her for an advantageous marriage. It would be a long time before girls had an equal chance of succeeding at school, but the principle that they had equal rights to education was gaining a secure foothold. What was still missing was any connection between their improving education and possible employment or careers.

Sarah Burton, Lydia's headmistress, is a feisty, independent woman. She clashes with the reactionary local authority as she battles for educational reforms. For her to rise to a position where she was running the school was a major career achievement. The role brought considerable social standing — similar to or even higher status than it does today — but significantly less financial reward. There was also another large bluebottle in the ointment: the marriage bar, which meant that any woman's teaching career would end on her wedding day. Not being allowed to combine professional and family life ruled hundreds of thousands of women out from any real career. In the book, Sarah wrestles with the incompatible pulls of career and emotional life.

Fast-forward another 70 years and I'm sitting in central London talking with Kirsten, a senior executive in her early 50s. Smart and confident, with a sense of calm about her, in some ways Kirsten embodies the changes that have occurred within education and employment: she did extremely well educationally, and has led a professional life. In other ways she is highly atypical, notably in her choice of subjects to study and in the career path she has followed.

Neither of Kirsten's parents had much of an educational background, though her father was a successful entrepreneur. She went to a girls' grammar school, but left at 16, after her GCSEs (General Certificate of Secondary Education) — 'I wasn't comfortable with that environment,' she says — and started on a technical apprenticeship, splitting her time between college and the workplace. It was a difficult phase: 'I worked on the machine-tool floor, a very male environment. The young men I was with were not particularly mature, and they teased me, sometimes even ostracised me. But I managed to stick with it. It makes you thick-skinned, contained, determined.'

She completed the apprenticeship in two years, and went straight on to study engineering at university — 'though I couldn't have done that today,' she is quick to tell me, 'because I didn't have the maths; I did that in my degree.' The only woman in a class of 150, she passed top of the group. From there, her career took off. She gained a place on a premier graduate programme at BP: high in kudos, training, and pay. 'BP was a great, open environment, but it was a pretty male environment again. I was working in the central London office. It was desk-based activity, evaluating new exploration prospects. There was no impediment at that stage to my development — very much the reverse: I got a lot of encouragement. But I wanted to work in a more operational environment and work towards being a plant manager, so I left and joined ICI [Imperial Chemical Industries] in the North East.'

She reached a senior management position while still in her 20s (the youngest person in the company to do so) and took over operational responsibility for central engineering at ICI's Runcorn plant, on the river Mersey. 'This was a very substantial responsibility, particularly as I was working with the unions in quite a confrontational context,' she recalls. (We are talking about the 1980s, when industrial relations in the United Kingdom were highly frictional, and strikes commonplace.) 'But I had a very good mentor who really wanted to give me the opportunities to develop.' So Kirsten continued to climb up the ladder, leaving Runcorn to move into a more commercial role within ICI, and becoming business manager for a global business unit.

Thus far, thus quite unusual. Women of Kirsten's generation were already making their way into higher education in large numbers, but not by the route she followed. Hardly any would have chosen engineering or related subjects, and even fewer — possibly none — would have had a career path as steep as hers.

Then her mentor left, and that had a big impact on her. Despite being an exceptionally determined, intelligent, and courageous woman, she had still found the presence of someone who could nurture her and her career extremely important. It was shortly afterwards that she took a career break, and had two children within two years. 'I came back in between them,' she told me, 'but when I came back it was more difficult, and I never really got back on to the career pathway. Now that my mentor had gone, I wasn't given — or else I couldn't find — what I'd describe as a proper job. ICI was shrinking. My new line manager was a commercial, not an operations, guy and didn't really understand what I was doing. If you don't have anyone who's speaking for you, you're lost.'

So she left ICI and, because she wanted to be working at board level, joined a smaller company as operations director. She relates with a sigh, 'It started okay, but the business was sold to a private equity company and I was effectively demoted. For a while I worked along with it, because it fitted my circumstances, with two small children. But the business was sold off in bits. The equity managers were male, and they ran it. I was useful to them, and I was rewarded fine, but I was not on the board. So, although it had started off really well, it didn't deliver my goal.'

In short, Kirsten was a woman, a production and operations person, and well capable of taking a board level role. She was faced by male private equity managers who were exclusively interested in balance sheets and who thought that a large pay package would be sufficient reward. It wasn't, and she left.

Kirsten now heads a sector skills body, still in the industry she loves. For the first time, she's managing an organisation with significant numbers of women in it. I ask her how she finds it. She taps her fingers reflectively as she repeats my question. 'How do I find it? In some respects for me it's actually been more difficult … Some of that is because my management style is more male than female — that's what I've grown up with. I've had to change quite a bit of how I manage, my leadership style, how I relate to the teams.'

How exactly? She hesitates. 'There are broadbrush differences, though there's a danger of stereotyping here! I actually find working with men more straightforward. Working with women, there are a lot more factors to take account of. It's a more holistic process to take account of all their needs. Men understand management by objectives. Women often need more of the other things, a different dialogue around what is expected of them, more of a depth of understanding about how they fit into the organisation. It's about a relationship, whereas men are more transactional.'

We'll meet Kirsten again when we look at the issue of choice (Chapter 8), but it's clear that many of the choices she has made are unconventional for a woman even today. Her story, atypical as it is, both symbolises the changes that have occurred since the days of Maggie and Lydia, and encapsulates many of the issues that still remain. She was a high achiever educationally, even though her choice of career is highly distinctive. Then her circumstances changed, and her skills were not being valued; she switched occupation, and is now altering her management style because of the palpable differences she has discovered in the ways women and men work. It's a parable of a kind for our time, sketched in primary colours.

Peter and Paula: mirror images

'Every employee tends to rise to his level of incompetence.' This is the Peter Principle, named after its creator, Laurence Peter. His book of the same name, co-authored with Raymond Hull, was a semi-humorous account — mainly a collection of stories, many partly fictionalised — of how and why people rise up organisational hierarchies.[7] Peter's insight was that employees go on being promoted for demonstrating competence at the job they are doing *until this is no longer the case*. So, he reasoned, they arrive at the level above the one at which they are really capable of performing — and this in turn accounts for much of the incompetence we encounter, at various levels, in organisations of different kinds. Peter provides numerous, often painfully recognisable, examples.

The 'his' of the Principle says to us today that the employees in Peter's firing line were men. In the 1960s, the pronoun would not have had the same gender-defining resonance; 'his' stood for everyone's. But it was in fact the case that the Peter Principle referred almost exclusively to men's promotions. Women were no longer simply disregarded in educational contexts, as Maggie Tulliver was; educational reformers continued to make efforts so that promising girls would not be lost to the system, as Lydia Holly was. Yet women's profile in the workplace was low to the point of invisibility.

The only woman to figure among Peter's examples is a Miss Totland, who as 'a competent student and an outstanding primary teacher, was promoted to primary supervisor. She now has to teach not children but teachers. Yet *she still uses the techniques which worked so well with small children* ... She speaks slowly and distinctly. She uses mostly words of one or two syllables. She explains each point several times in different ways, to be sure it is understood. She always wears a bright smile.'[8] It's not hard to see why the ever-smiling and simple-worded Miss Totland did not flourish as a supervisor of adult teachers; the competences that made her such a good teacher of small children did not transfer well to her promoted role as a trainer of adults.

'The Peter Principle' went viral. The book itself sold several million copies, and was reissued on its 40th birthday — a rare accolade. But it was not so much the book's sales or readership that registered its fame; it was the entry of the Principle into common parlance, as people the world over recognised how it chimed with their own experience. For several decades, 'the Peter Principle' has been a familiar phrase to many who have never read the book.[9]

The Peter Principle challenged all kinds of assumptions, especially that we live in a world where competent performance is efficiently recognised and fairly rewarded by promotion, regardless of irrelevant factors such as what sex or ethnicity you are. Reflecting the nature of most employment in the 1960s, its main reference points were hierarchical organisations with well-defined career paths, where people — men — step their way steadily upwards. The Peter Principle caught on so well mainly because it gave a neat label, and a simple explanation, for the kinds of egregious incompetence that are familiar to anyone who has worked in organisations, and that blow such a big hole in the complacent assumption that a meritocratic system actually exists. Most of us can all too easily come up with at least one or two examples of our own to add to Peter's list — or may even fear that we embody the Principle ourselves. One way or another, the Peter Principle still provokes a chuckle, a sigh of recognition, or a rueful shake of the head.

The Paula Principle is in essence the Peter Principle's mirror image. It holds that 'most women work below their level of competence'. Around the industrialised world, women emerge from education systems better qualified than they have ever been; they are better qualified than men; and the competence gap is increasing.[10] As adults, women are more disposed than men to carry on learning at work, acquiring new skills and adding further to this competence gap. Yet they do not see this reflected by our reward systems, in their earnings or in their careers. True, the average earnings gap between men and women has been narrowing over time. It is also true that more women are finding their way up career ladders. We have many more female professionals, such as doctors and lawyers, than 20 years ago; more women managers; and more women in positions of power at different levels. But this is no steady progression: it is happening very unevenly, much more slowly than the increase in their competences would lead us to expect, and, on occasion, the process is actually thrown into reverse. Above all, for women who are not in professional jobs, receiving an equal reward for their competences is still further away than it is for their more highly educated sisters. Is this persistent contrast between competence and reward an anomaly, a paradox, or a scandal? Whatever you call it, it is the focus of the Paula Principle.

Both Principles are, of course, not universal truths but generalisations, and broad ones at that. Paula complements Peter directly, in two ways. First, I've already noted that Dr Peter expressed himself as if only men were working, or at least only men were involved in career pathways and promotions. The Paula Principle focuses on what is now fully the other half of the working population. In the United States, women outnumber men as jobholders. In the United Kingdom and Australia, women make up over 45% of the workforce. Across other countries that are members of the Organisation for Economic Co-operation and Development (OECD) — that is, the more industrialised world — the figures are mostly very similar.[11] Women seek, not surprisingly, employment that reflects their increasing qualifications and experience, and this applies at all levels, not only to the highly educated, who expect professional careers.

The second obvious complementarity is that Peter focused on men's arrival *above* their competence level. The Paula Principle focuses attention on why women tend to work *below* the level that they might expect to attain, given their qualifications and skills. It swings the argument around, to concentrate our gaze on the other side of the competence axis. The two Principles are intertwined, and interdependent. Reducing the effect of one will do the same for the other.

The Paula Principle reveals two things that should concern us all: a persistent *unfairness* or injustice in the way education is rewarded; and a *waste* of proven talent. Each of these has its own complexities. My take on the fairness question may not fit altogether comfortably with some widely held assumptions about gender equality. First, in education and training, gender inequality is seen not in terms of equality of opportunity but in the rewards that do or do not flow from male and female achievements. By 'rewards' I don't mean only financial returns, but also the other personal benefits associated with using one's talents to the full: satisfaction from knowing that one's abilities are being properly employed, and a sense of progression, of moving forward, whether or not this is in a conventional 'career'. Being valued is about more than the size of the salary or pay package. Since women's competences are increasing at a faster rate than the pay and careers gaps are closing, simple numerical equality, whether in pay or in positions attained, is no longer the appropriate measure. As we saw, this is something that Kirsten felt strongly.

Second, I argue that we need to see equality in a more dynamic way that does not focus only on individual times in women's working lives, but on *how opportunity is distributed over their lives as a whole*. This puts a different perspective on equality and fairness. Concentrating on symmetry between women and men at any single given age or stage in life is not the best way to frame the issue. For young women with a good educational record, the Paula Principle may seem no longer to apply: the pay gap for them is likely to be minimal, and most options are open to them.[12] But will this parity last as they get older? Almost certainly not, on current form. Women's career paths are flatter and more broken, their salaries lower, and their retirement incomes smaller. This is changing, but we need to see how things play out across all ages and stages, for each generation in turn, before we can get a true handle on equality.

The fairness argument therefore involves several dimensions. By contrast, the waste of talent seems a comparatively straightforward issue to grasp, if not to solve. The fact that many women are working below their competence level hurts them, personally and financially. It also hurts organisations, public and private, and the wider society.[13] If for the individual woman it means a lifelong income penalty, then for us collectively it means a lifelong efficiency and productivity penalty.

The UK Women & Work Commission estimated back in 2006 that simply increasing women's employment rates would add £15–23 billion to the economy. In the United States, raising the participation rate of women aged 25 to 54 in all states to that of the top 10 states (84%) would add 5.1 million women to the workforce — equivalent to adding 3–4% to the size of the US economy. A more recent global analysis of gender equality concluded that if all countries matched the rate of improvement of the fastest-improving country in their region, this could add as much as $12 trillion, or 11%, in annual 2025 GDP.[14]

Estimates of this kind are obviously subject to immense variation. If anything, however, they understate the issue because they focus only on what would happen if more women did paid work; they say nothing about what a better match between their competences and their jobs would mean once they are in work. In 2015, the UK government's consultation on closing the gender pay gap estimated that rewarding women's productivity and employment to the same financial levels as men's could add almost £600 billion to the economy.[15] If people — women especially — can put their talents to fuller use, there are huge gains to be made all round, for organisations as well as individuals. The worse the alignment between competences and jobs, the more public and private organisations are losing out on the potential benefits of skills and innovation.

More broadly, it really is likely that better decisions — commercial or political — would be made if those making them had a more appropriate representation of men and women.[16] (The same argument applies to ethnic minorities, and other under-represented groups; many other points in this book are relevant to them, too.) Avoiding groupthink and herd behaviour is easier to do with a more diverse and balanced staff. With a better gender balance at senior levels in our financial institutions, we might not have had the testosterone-fuelled financial crash of 2008. That is of course speculation (also indulged in by the head of the International Monetary Fund, Christine Lagarde, when she commented wryly on what might have happened if Lehman Brothers had been Lehman Sisters), but it is not implausible, and we all — or almost all — have an interest in avoiding any more of that kind of event.

To these costs we must add the ones that cannot have even an approximate financial value attached to them. Women who cannot fulfil their potential for no other reason than that they are women will, like anyone else, tend to feel frustration and resentment. If their own wellbeing is lower, it's reasonable to think this will affect their families, including their children, if they have any. These effects can be significant and lasting, even if they cannot easily be quantified into currency signs. In short, the Paula Principle raises important questions about how we 'value' and reward work of all kinds.

The argument about talent loss leads us into some quite tricky terrain. How is 'talent' defined, and by whom? Who decides what is 'valuable', and what are the mechanisms for rewarding it? The market often has a large part to play in this, but 'the market' is not some independent and objective mechanism. It is a set of procedures and processes that are at least partly shaped by flesh-and-blood people, with their own values and interests. These are, to some extent inevitably, self-reproducing and self-reinforcing.

Take a look at the make-up of the remuneration committees that decide senior executive pay and you'll get the point. A 2012 survey of 96 FTSE top 100 companies showed that, of the 366 non-executive directors who sit on remuneration committees, just 37 were not from senior business levels themselves. This may seem natural enough, but as the report observes: 'Pay is a very sensitive subject, which is freighted with notions of worth, and personal value. Non-executive directors are often peers of the executives involved and it is hard to argue that rewards should be lower.'[17] In other words, the remunerators have a subconscious tendency to favour existing reward systems, with a built-in ratchet effect that boosts top incomes for people of their own ilk. It is not surprising that 45% of the companies have all-male remuneration committees, and women make up only 16% of the total number of persons serving on these committees. Remuneration committees deal only with senior staff, but the divergence of perception on what is valuable operates at all levels. 'Value' has different meanings for different people.

The Paula Principle is new as a label, but the issue that underlies it is not. Arguably it has been around ever since competent women have been under-rewarded — in other words, probably forever. Certainly it was already operating back in the 1960s, despite Peter's indifference to gender. Many women then got nowhere near the grades of job that they would have carried out with full competence, given the chance. This was true both within occupations — they could not climb vertically up organisational hierarchies — and because they were excluded from many occupations in the first place. So a woman probably could not become a train driver, lawyer, or engineer; and, even if she could, she should certainly not aspire to become a partner or a supervisor.

The mismatch was (and is) not only about promotions but also about the content of the job. In all kinds of workplaces, women were patently able beyond the requirements of their jobs. Anyone who, as I did, worked in an office more than 30 years ago will recall the sheer volume of fairly mindless repetitive copy-typing required before word processors arrived. This was done almost exclusively by women whose intelligences far exceeded that required for the job (and not infrequently that of their bosses). Nowadays, those same women would have advanced qualifications and professional expectations.[18] The factors that explain this, such as discrimination, unaffordable childcare, and lack of self-belief, which I describe in Chapters 4, 5, and 6, still underpin the current version of the Paula Principle, but they carry very different weightings today than they did 40 years ago. Some of them have diminished. Others loom as large as, or larger than, ever. In short, across the developed world, between Peter articulating his principle and Paula emerging from the shadows, we have seen much change but by no means enough.

Three other comparative observations and then I shall largely wave the Peter Principle goodbye. First, neither the Peter nor the Paula Principle is a statement of the inevitable. Far from it. The 'principle' is a tendency that reflects current norms and practices; by bringing the Paula Principle into the spotlight, even if mainly by virtue of its name, I hope to help diminish its power. Most (though not all) of the factors that underpin it are negative ones — social obstacles to be overcome.

Second, bracketing Peter and Paula naturally triggers the question of whether Peter will be 'robbed' to pay Paula. If women get to exercise their competences more fully, does this mean that men will lose out? The whole thrust of my argument is that everyone should be given due opportunity to exercise their skills to the full. Given that women are now acquiring skills and qualifications at a faster rate than men, any self-respecting and genuinely meritocratic system would have them occupy more of the positions that demand those skills, and so move up ladders ahead of less-well-qualified men. End of zero-sum story: justice will have been served, and robbery does not come into it. However, the story need not be so bluntly zero-sum. On the contrary: men as well as women should gain, since enabling more women to make better use of their skills will improve the performance of individual organisations, occupational sectors, and the economy as a whole. The more that is done about the effects of the Paula Principle, the less likely we are to suffer the effects of the Peter Principle. This means that some men will not get promotions they might otherwise have got. But more women will find new, higher positions than men will be displaced — not a complete win-win, but a positive, rather than a zero-sum game. The damage to male chances will not be nearly as severe as a simple levelling up/down implies.[19]

Lastly, the Paula Principle applies, as the Peter Principle did (and maybe still does), to all occupational levels, and emphatically not just to professionals, managers, and other senior ranks. In the debate on gender equality at work, there is a natural tendency to focus on the top jobs: on how few women are judges, CEOs, cabinet ministers, and so on. Facebook's boss Sheryl Sandberg's advice to women to 'lean in' — to sustain involvement in leadership roles — is one of the best-known phrases in the debate.[20] It comes from an exceptional woman and is mainly aimed at those with very high career aspirations. Concentrating on the glass ceiling is understandable, and justifiable in that inequality at this level reflects the structure of power most acutely. People in top jobs are the ones who wield most influence,[21] and so we should be most interested in how these kinds of job are distributed between women and men, as well as across other social categories. But this excludes the great majority of women, for whom the glass ceiling is not an image that ever resonates (see Chapter 3). The Paula Principle applies as much to the clerk who does not apply for a supervisor's job because she does not have the confidence, or to the nursery assistant who cannot progress to a more senior level because taking a full-time job would mean losing more in childcare costs than she would gain in salary, as it does to the vice-president or deputy CEO blocked from the top job by covert discrimination or male cliquery. It is a system-wide — or, rather, system-deep — principle, not one focused on the top layers only.

This is what we shall be going on to explore. But first we shall take a closer look at how women have overtaken men in education and skills, and why this is significant for our story.

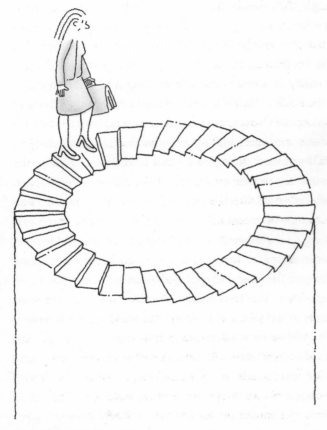

The impossible career path

2

Educated Rita

How women have overtaken men in education and skills

At almost every level, in almost every subject, and in almost every developed country, women have overtaken men in education, and the gap is widening. Quite why there has not been more comment on this transformation is a puzzle, to me at least, especially since the switch in the relative educational achievements of women and men is remarkably similar and pronounced across all advanced economies.

My aim in this chapter is to provide a sense of the *trajectories* involved in getting to where we are now. While this may not tell us what will happen next (as scientist Niels Bohr said, 'Prediction is very difficult — especially about the future'), tracing out these crossovers brings into sharp relief the lag between change in educational achievement and progress in careers and income.

We would not expect the effects of the educational crossovers to be instantaneous. These kinds of change take time for their effects to be felt. The question is, how long is it reasonable to wait? Is it just a matter of biding time till the crossover weaves its way into the workplace? Or have its effects somehow been subverted — corralled into blind alleys or running into buffers? The sense I want to convey is of a dynamic process whose effects — on women, men, and society as a whole — have not at all percolated through into the world of work as fully as we might have expected. There are political choices involved in whether and how we recognise this major change in the educational landscape. The Paula Principle is not an iron law but is open to action and modification.

In some cases, we can pinpoint a specific crossover moment when women overtook men in their educational trajectories — whether in *participation* rates (for example, the proportions of women and men entering higher education), or in the *qualifications* gained by women and men at different levels (that is, whether they succeed as students). In reality, the exact crossover point is fairly meaningless — it is not as if there was a vote to be won by whichever sex could muster 50% +1. Yet such a moment carries a strong symbolic charge, and in that sense is, indeed, meaningful. It also establishes a base point from which we can compare the rewards that flow to women and men from their educational achievements.

Before going any further, I have to stress the obvious but basic fact that women and men are not two homogeneous groups. Students of gender constantly point out that there are much greater differences between women than between women and men. In the educational profiles of women (and men), there are striking differences between social classes, ethnic groups, and age groups, to name but three. So gender differences should not be exalted unhelpfully; this seems to me a fundamental argument against simple numerical — 50/50 — equality as a goal (see Chapter 4).[1]

The Paula Principle, very evidently, addresses only one form of social divide. Between social classes in particular there is a huge variation in achievement, from early years onwards. Girls from lower socio-economic backgrounds trail way behind those who begin in more advantaged circumstances. A well-off Paula is almost certain to do better educationally than a poor Paula, and the gap between the achievements of those two is likely to be far bigger than between a poor Paula and a poor Peter, or a well-off Paula and well-off Peter.

Moreover, the gap between women from well-off family backgrounds and those from poorer backgrounds is increasing, rather than reducing. Class trumps gender when it comes to understanding education and its outcomes.

We can get a flavour of this from the stories of Iona, Vanessa, and Mandy, three women from the North East of England whose similar educational trajectories represent their generation quite accurately. They went to school in the 1970s. For none of them did it bring much benefit.

Iona was born into a working-class family, which she describes as dysfunctional. 'Education, I would say, wasn't a great priority … basically I wasn't encouraged. The culture I came from, I don't think anyone went to university, the women just got married.' She pauses and sighs. 'I might have it wrong, but I think if you come from a family with enlightened parents, I think women might do as well as men. I'm sure I wasn't 15 when I left school …' She breaks off and frowns. 'Or was I just 15? I can't remember. Would you have been allowed to start work before 15?'

In any event, Iona left school one Friday and started stacking shelves in a supermarket on the following Monday. After that came work in a bakery in Doncaster and a fish-processing factory in North Shields. Feeling restless, she seized the opportunity to take a job in a hotel in Germany, but it was only short term, and, reluctantly, having taking a liking to life in the nation, she returned home. Next she found work in a small printing press at the end of her road and married a co-worker there, whom she persuaded to take a job back in Germany. But by the time they moved, they had a small baby. This meant Iona was trapped at home with little support, and started to feel homesick. The marriage broke up when they moved back to the United Kingdom.

Vanessa also left school at 15 with no qualifications, and went straight into a job in the textile industry. She married at 20 and had three children. She had a job in a supermarket for many years, until the kids all began school, and then joined the civil service, working in the tax office. Her children typify the trend in the next generation: her daughter has gone to university, and is now energetically pursuing a career as a political journalist. By contrast, Vanessa's two boys got reasonable results at school, but neither went on to college. One has a job but is still at home, aged 28; the other has moved out and works in a bar.

As for Mandy, the last of the trio, she actually got good exam results at school, but her parents took the view that girls don't go to college. They had a factory job lined up for her, but she chose a position for herself, as a telephonist for a music company, and then became an office junior for a company that repaired industrial cleaners. She was married at 18 and soon had two children. 'Anyone who went for careers advice who was working class, it was, "Why don't you become a hairdresser or work in a kitchen?" You know, jobs that didn't go anywhere,' she recalls ruefully.

We'll meet these three women again; they all found their way back into education, as did many women of their era who had not fulfilled anything like their potential in their initial period of schooling. In those days, hardly anyone paused to regret the early departure of women such as Iona, Vanessa, and Mandy from the education system. There are still many young women whose lives follow a very similar pattern, but, fortunately, far fewer than there used to be. The expectations have changed, as a look at who does well in schools, colleges, and higher education shows us.

The great educational divide

Willy Russell's play *Educating Rita* has cult status among adult educators of a certain generation. Set in the 1970s, it tracks the development of Rita, a working-class hairdresser from Liverpool with a powerful Scouse humour. Her cultural background has not encouraged educational success: 'Studying was just for the wimps, wasn't it? See, if I'd started takin' school seriously I would have had to become different from me mates, an' that's not allowed ... Like what you've got to be into is music an' clothes an' looking for a feller, y' know, the real qualities of life.'[2]

At 26, she becomes frustrated with the limitations of her culture and finds her way onto an Open University course. It brings her into contact with Frank, a middle-class alcoholic university lecturer who is supposed to tutor her:

Rita: Do you get a lot of students like me?

Frank: Not exactly, no ...

Rita: I was dead surprised when they took me. I don't suppose they would have done if it'd been a proper university. The OU's different though, isn't it?[3]

Rita never lacks confidence, or at least never seems to, but at the beginning she has no grasp of what is expected with university study, despite her evident intelligence. The real issue, though, is one of cultural adaptation. She stops working as a hairdresser and takes a job in a 'bistro' (which at the time symbolised middle-class consumption tastes). As the play progresses, Frank moves from patronising her to taking her seriously, while she moves in the opposite direction, from deference to his learning to anger at his clumsy attempts to exercise control:

'I'll tell you what you can't bear, Mr Self-Pitying Piss-Artist; what you can't bear is that I am educated now. What's up, Frank, don't you like me now that the little girl's grown up, now that you can no longer bounce me on Daddy's knee an' watch me stare back in wide-eyed wonder at everything he has to say? I'm educated, I've got what you have an' you don't like it.'[4]

There were quite a few Ritas in the 1970s, if not so many with her crackle: adult women with some schooling who had never had the opportunity to progress beyond that. For the Paula Principle, there is a further relevance in the play's plot. Rita's husband, Denny, wants her to stay home, have babies, and content herself with traditional working-class habits and roles — epitomised, to Russell, by pub sing-alongs with the family. Denny is appalled at her idea of bettering herself. Unsurprisingly, as she progresses further in her education, she leaves him.

The gap in academic achievement starts at school.

There are many more Ritas than Dennys in adult classes. In the mid-1990s, there was a gap of 5% in favour of men. Fifteen years later, this had been reversed. The Department for Business, Innovation, and Skills carried out a large-scale survey of those involved in community learning, and found a 3:1 ratio in favour of women: no fewer than 76% of the adult learners were female. The crossover point occurred somewhere around the turn of the millennium.[5] No fireworks, but an important moment. In fact, across Europe as a whole, more women take up adult education annually — 9.6% compared with 8.2% of men (about a 20% gap) in 2011. In the countries that are generally thought to lead the way on gender equality, the gap is much bigger. (It is unlikely, by the way, to be a coincidence that the countries that are strongest on gender equality also show the highest rates of adult learning. In Denmark, Sweden, and Finland, participation rates are above 20%, and women are out ahead of men — in Denmark's case, by a striking 13 percentage points.)[6]

While men are also doing better than they used to educationally, their upward gradient is a very gentle one compared to that of their sisters. It is a remarkably consistent pattern internationally: the educational crossovers — women overtaking men — have happened in all of the 30-plus countries that belong to the OECD. They reflect broad social trends over the past half-century: an end to crude assumptions about female abilities and aspirations, greater attention to the kinds of pedagogy that give equal chances to young women, and an acceptance of women's aspirations for fulfilling work outside the home. Across the OECD, an average of 76% of girls complete their upper secondary education, compared with 68% of boys. In some countries, such as Norway and Israel, the gap is around 15 percentage points. (The United Kingdom is notably below the average OECD level, at 72% and 63%.)[7] At college and university level, women are outdoing men in almost every OECD country. In 1985, 46% of women graduates in OECD countries were women. The situation has now completely reversed, and 57% of first-time tertiary graduates are women.[8] Australia, the United States, and the United Kingdom are all at this average. The pattern is blindingly clear across countries that have already modernised; even in those with more gender-traditional cultures, such as Turkey, more than half of tertiary graduates are women. It is not — yet — true for poorer countries in other parts of the world, but I would bet a lot of money that it will be so quite soon for most of them.

This is leading to a distinctly asymmetrical scenario. As the OECD publication *Closing the Gender Gap* points out: 'If this trend continues, there will be an average of 1.4 female students for every male student by 2025, and almost twice as many women in tertiary education in Austria, Canada, Iceland, Norway and the United Kingdom'.[9] Remember that this does not reflect any drop in men's enrolments, just that the increase in women's is so much steeper. Judging by current patterns of graduation, about 46% of women and 31% of men in OECD countries today will complete higher education at some point in their lives. This is a huge gap.

The subject divide

So the tide has been running strongly in favour of female achievement for many years now — and it shows no signs of turning. But the broad trend does not apply across all subjects. Men still go into sciences and maths in much more significant numbers, despite constant efforts to encourage more women into these subjects. In every OECD country except Turkey and Mexico, men graduate in sciences in far greater numbers than women. The converse is, of course, true to an even greater extent: there are far, far more women graduating in arts and social-science subjects. This matters for the Paula Principle.

In some respects, subject segregation seems to be getting stronger; the proportion of women among computer graduates in OECD countries actually fell between 2000 and 2009. The subject imbalance is important not only because it suggests that women and men are still channelled into different subject areas, limiting their choices. Science graduates earn more than their arts and social-science counterparts, mainly because their qualifications open up routes into jobs in the private sector, and these on average pay better than those in the public or voluntary sector. In the United States, nine of the top 10 'earners' after graduation were in technology — computer engineers could expect to earn an average of $70,400 on graduation, closely followed by chemical engineers at $66,400.[10] If women do not go into these areas, that has a strong material effect on their lifetime earnings.

As an aside: a surprising fact is that philosophy is closer to science subjects in gender bias than to the rest of the humanities, with which it is usually associated. In the United Kingdom in 2009, 45% of all philosophy undergraduates and postgraduates were women — a figure closer to the 40% in maths than to the 58% in history, and a very long way indeed from the 73% found in the English department.[11] I find this interesting for a mix of epistemological and cultural reasons (quite apart from the fact that one of my daughters is studying the subject): is philosophy intrinsically more akin to subjects such as maths in an intellectual sense — and does this go along with a certain style of argument or behaviour that discourages women?[12] I wonder how Socrates would have answered the question.

The first crossover point

Paula learns earlier and faster than Peter, as she may always have done. Once, when giving the Paula Principle its first public outing, I asked a conference audience for their views on why this should be. We were in Vienna and the first response was suitably Freudian: that girls have more of an inbuilt tendency to wish to please authority figures such as teachers and parents, and so apply themselves more. (As a father of two daughters, I have my own thoughts on this, but wouldn't dream of imposing these on anyone.) The simple fact that girls mature earlier than boys will certainly have quite a lot to do with it.

Let's turn to look at our first significant crossover point — the school leaving certificate or international baccalaureate, which is the dominant qualification for entry into higher education and thereafter into a professional career. In the United Kingdom (or, more precisely, England), this means A levels or their equivalent. Girls were already outperforming boys in the 1960s, but many of them left school at the earliest opportunity and so didn't get to take A levels. It wasn't until this waste of talent became recognised in the 1970s that girls started staying on in much greater numbers — in itself a symbol of the wider change in attitudes to gender roles. As a result, although the rate of change was quite gradual, girls overtook boys in A-level grades a full quarter of a century ago.

The gap has increased steadily ever since. A whopping 78,000 more females than males got some kind of A level in England in 2015. Of these, 11,077 women attained the top grades — A* or A — compared with 8,184 men. The only apparent exception to the overall pattern is the proportion of boys getting the very top A* grade — 9.0% compared with 8.1% for the girls. But the figure is a *proportion*, and does not signal equality: since so many more girls take A levels, the *absolute* number of A* is still smaller for boys — 3,069 compared to 3,377. At the other end of the scale, more boys got nothing or just a minimal grade, both in absolute numbers and proportionately. One in four males (137,000) got the lowest grades (D or below), compared with one in five females (83,000).[13]

The same pattern broadly holds true in other countries, with their different grading systems. In Australia's New South Wales, for example, girls came 'top of course' in 70% of the subjects examined for the High School Certificate in 2015. Every year at exam-result time, newspapers publish pictures of girls whooping with delight —

possibly just because newspapers like to show girls, or because girls show their delight more photogenically than boys, but whatever the reason, there are definitely more of them available to celebrate.

The second crossover point

Now we turn to what counts most when it comes to getting good jobs — and which might be expected to be reflected clearly in the careers and pay of those who do well: courses leading to degrees and diplomas in either community education colleges (further education) or universities (higher education).

UK Attendances in Full-time Further and Higher Education Since 1970/71

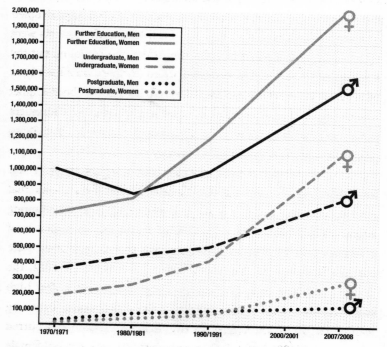

The crossovers in university and college education in England and Wales.
Source: author's analysis of data from the UK Office for National Statistics.

The graph on page 28 shows the trend in higher and further education in the United Kingdom. Forty years ago, women were well behind men in every single category, with less than 75% of the male enrolments in further education, and less than 50% of male enrolments in higher education, sinking to less than one-third at postgraduate level. Ten years later, in 1980, they had overtaken men in full-time further education, but were still well behind elsewhere. By 1990, they were in the majority in further education overall — that is, combining full- and part-time — but still trailed in higher education, though the gap at undergraduate level had narrowed significantly.

Since then, although men have gone to colleges and universities in increasing numbers, the trajectory for women has been significantly steeper. While the number of men enrolled in full-time undergraduate university courses roughly doubled, the number of women quadrupled. At postgraduate levels, the numbers of full-time male students went up by 150%, and of part-timers by almost the same amount; but the numbers of women tripled and quadrupled. In short, men have been piling into higher education at all levels, but there has been a quiet whooshing noise as women shoot past them in far greater numbers. In further education, the angle of divergence is currently not quite so steep, but women now outnumber men by more than 20%.

The same picture emerges very clearly in other countries. A Pew Research Center analysis of US Census Bureau data shows that 'females outpace males in college enrollment, especially among Hispanics and blacks. In 1994, 63% of recent female high-school graduates and 61% of male recent high-school graduates were enrolled in college in the fall following graduation. By 2012, the share of young women enrolled in college immediately after high school had increased to 71%, but it remained unchanged for young men at 61%.' In Australia, the crossover in higher education occurred as long ago as 1987. In 2014, there were just 80 males per 100 female students in higher education.

There is, to be sure, some artificiality in the UK figures. Part of the big jump in female higher education enrolments happened when degrees in nursing were introduced, bringing thousands of additional women but very few men into university study. Other professions, such as occupational therapy, have also followed down the degree-seeking path, transferring their — largely female — student bodies into higher education. But this does not undermine the overall picture to any significant extent.

Just because people start degrees, it doesn't necessarily mean that they get the qualification. In UK higher education, people accepted into a degree course generally complete it and get their degree. The overall drop-out rate is low, but even so it is men who are more likely to drop out than women, especially at higher levels of qualification.[14] So we can be pretty sure that these enrolments translate into effective qualifications, with a growing female–male gap.

But there are degrees and there are degrees. Even if fewer men than women are getting university qualifications, are they more likely to get the top ones when they do — the first-class honours or the *summa cum laudes*? They used to, naturally, when there were more men in higher education. Various reasons were given for this — for instance, that men were more prepared to take the kinds of intellectual risk that really lights up the examiners' eyes. Not any more. Once enrolled, a man is still very marginally more likely than a woman to get a first-class degree but, as with school-leaving results, this is a matter of proportion, not an absolute. Because so many more women graduate overall, more women than men leave with first-class degrees — if we take the United Kingdom as an example, the figures are 39,270 against 30,135 in 2015.[15] The trend is similar in Australia.

In the main, it is only important to have a first-class degree if you want a career in academia or research. For all other careers, getting an upper second is nearly as good — and women excel here, too: in the United Kingdom, 70% of them leave university with a first-class or upper-second-class degree, compared with 65% of men. This boils down to 40,000 more women than men leaving higher education every year with a qualification high enough to lead to a 'graduate job' — whatever the frailties of that as a concept.

On top of this, at the peak of our academic pyramid, as many women as men take up full-time postgraduate education, and are way ahead of men in part-time enrolments. Men still get more doctorates (4,500 against 4,225 in 2009/10 in the United Kingdom[16]) but there is no doubt that, overall, higher academic qualifications are going increasingly to women. There are many more Master Paulas than Master Peters emerging from our universities.

What about elites?

There is one other feature of the landscape that needs attention, especially when the argument is to do with power and how it is distributed. Have women, for all their numerical superiority, been channelled into lower-status universities? The same question could be asked of any country with a stratified higher education system, such as the United States, with its Ivy League, or France, with its *grandes écoles*.

Britain, where I live and work, is severely stratified into social and educational layers. Universities do a mixed job on this class layering: they give some a wonderful chance to move up, but they also reinforce the stratification, as they sort and sift people into universities or colleges with very different levels of status, reputation, and subsequent reward. The United Kingdom has the so-called Russell Group (attracting elites and very keen on research), heavily marked out from the Million+ group (proudly catering for students from so-called non-traditional backgrounds) and other clusters of non-elite institutions with different profiles. Some of the forces that have propelled women's numbers upwards push them in the latter direction; for example, nursing degrees do not figure strongly in Russell Group universities. Elite universities tend to eschew the newer types of courses, such as estate management or sports sciences, which have emerged as part of the overall expansion of higher education. But women have not been corralled into lower-status universities, and with some subject exceptions their success permeates the higher education system at all its many levels.

On the contrary, the elite Paulas have overtaken the elite Peters. In 1995/96, 11% more men had enrolled for first degrees in Russell Group universities. Just seven years later, the crossover had already happened, and by 2011/12 the gap had exactly reversed, to 11% in favour of women. At Master's level, the switch was even greater, from 31% more men in 1995 to a 17% lead for women in 2011.

These are dramatic reversals. The total enrolment gap between women and men at the UK's elite universities is now more than 20%. If we exclude non-UK students, the gap gets even wider, to well over 25%. But you already know the punchline: success in elite education has not translated into success in elite positions at work.

Here, in summary, are the key crossover points in the context of England and Wales.[17] The tidal wave started a long way back and has been rolling on ever since.

1981: Women overtake men in FE participation
1989: Girls overtake boys in getting 2+ A levels
1993: Higher female participation in training
1994: Women overtake men in HE participation
1999: Ditto in Russell Group undergraduates
2005: Ditto in Russell Group graduates

The direction of the narrative is undeniable. At every level in the formal education system, women are now outperforming men, and in almost every subject. In almost any occupation, and at almost every level in which formal qualifications count, women are more likely to have them. Males are thinner on the top of the qualifications pyramid, and more heavily weighted towards the bottom. Remarkably similar profiles prevail in most developed countries.

A glimpse of the global picture

What is the picture elsewhere, beyond the rich countries of the OECD? Here the position of girls and women is very different. Twenty years ago, women from the world's nations gathered under the auspices of the UN to issue the Beijing Declaration on equality, with education and training a major theme.[18] There is now a global current flowing towards redressing the huge imbalances between the sexes at school, and reducing illiteracy among adult women. But the flow has not settled into an even pattern in all countries, and in poorer countries it is especially turbulent.

Let's just get some brief takes on the issue, drawing from information supplied by the UNESCO Institute of Statistics:

- In many of the poorest countries, mainly Sub-Saharan Africa, girls still lag far behind. Among the many millions of children who never make it to school, there are always more girls than boys. There is very broad consensus that high priority should be given to enabling girls to realise their educational potential as a central factor in development.[19] A simple estimate underlines graphically how much this matters: a 1% rise in women's literacy is three times more likely to reduce deaths in children than an equivalent rise in the number of doctors.[20] The problem is converting the consensus into action.
- Across the globe, adult literacy rates show variable movement. Around 1990, there was a 13-point difference in global adult

literacy rates for men and women, with male literacy estimated at 82% and female at 69%. A decade later, the gap had shrunk to nine points — from 89% to 80%. There is much regional variation: in Latin American and Caribbean countries, there is already gender parity in adult literacy; in Middle Eastern and North African countries, there has been especially rapid progress in adult literacy for women, without yet reaching parity; but Sub-Saharan Africa remains with low levels, both relative to other countries and in women's literacy compared to men's. The great majority of the more than 700 million people with low literacy are women.[21]

- Other countries already well down the path of economic development do not have a common pattern. For example, in Russia, the gap in favour of women in tertiary education is already very large, at 22.8 points, but in India, the crossover has not yet happened. In China, the female share of undergraduate enrolments in regular higher education went up from 44% in 2002 to 48% in 2006. Chinese women overtook men in 2008, and by 2011 had more than 51% of the total (11.8 million versus 11.3 million). By 2020, China will be supplying nearly 30% of the world's graduates aged 25 to 34; as with most global statistics, the trend in that country alone will shape the whole picture.

We can see from this that educational crossovers have already occurred at several levels of education in many parts of the world. They have yet to be connected to the workplace and to concerns about equality of pay — the Paula Principle obviously does not yet apply in many of these countries, in part because far fewer women work in paid employment. But it is a fair bet that it will in years to come, and as women catch up and pass men in educational participation, country by country, the issues the Principle raises will begin to show themselves.

Educational effort: Makula's story

I may have given the impression that educational crossovers have come about naturally. Indeed, for some women it has been quite a smooth ride; they have had most of the formal obstacles removed from their path. But others have had to work extremely hard, in punishing circumstances, to achieve their results.

Makula is Ugandan. She works in London, at a hostel for disabled people. She is a diligent churchgoer, and at weekends helps to run a crèche for her church. Last year she was able to return to Uganda for the first time in nine years, to see her two sons, who were seven and 16 when she left.

Makula started well at school. 'But when I reached the end of primary, my dad said he didn't have any more money. My brother said he would go and earn money so I could stay on. Sadly, he passed away — he was so keen that I should carry on studying.' She sighs at the memory. 'When I reached the end of S2 [second year at secondary school], my father said he didn't have any more money, so I worked and paid for myself to go on to S4. But then I got pregnant, so I stopped. I felt I had let myself down.'

Makula got a job in a daycare centre. 'I've always been good with children, perhaps because I had to look after my siblings. A woman who had a child at the centre asked me to go travelling with her. Then they wanted to go to the US, and it was difficult for me to go in and out with the visa.' So Makula stayed in the United Kingdom, and took work as a cleaner. 'For five to six years, I just did cleaning. I was waking up at 4.00 am to do the cleaning jobs, starting work at 5.00 am. But I was starting to get tired, so I started to train as a carer and then I found a job as a support worker in a home for people with physical difficulties. It's full-time; I started working in the day, but because I wanted to take a course I asked to switch to nights. With the night job, you put them to bed, give them medication, check them every two hours, give them water as required. In the morning, you get a few of them up, bath them, dress them. Then you write the reports. It's 48 hours — or is it 38?' Makula has to pause to work it out. It turns out to be four shifts of 12 hours each. After finishing her shifts, she regularly goes on to do cleaning jobs for several households. This includes mine, where she arrives with a rucksack full of her Open University coursework.

The OU course is on childcare. She gets out the books, and we discuss how she will tackle her assignments. Makula has very successfully completed the first year, and is now aiming to finish the diploma. It will have been hard earned, and I am full of admiration for her.

And the gap will widen

When it comes to future intentions of learning, it looks as if this trend will be reinforced. In 2005, nearly as many men as women said they were likely or very likely to take part in some form of learning. By 2011, men's intentions had weakened while women's held steady at 40%, six points higher. If both sexes mean what they say — and who knows how far this is ever the case — then the divergence will increase further, as women carry on learning but men slide out of the door (or rather, never make it into the adult classroom in the first place).

There are still barriers that discourage both women and men from taking part in education and training. If we are interested in encouraging adult learning — and I am — the reasons for this are important, and relevant to the Paula Principle. More than in any other country, men in the United Kingdom cite working hours as a factor that discourages them from taking up learning (presumably other than learning undertaken in work time). About one in three British men gives this as a reason. Of course, they may just be finding an excuse for themselves, but a workplace culture of long hours does take its toll on ability to find time for learning. Another one in five gives family responsibilities as a factor. For women, on the other hand, it is family responsibilities that are to the fore. In the United Kingdom, women cite childcare and similar responsibilities more than women in any other comparably sized countries, and far more often than in the benchmark Scandinavian countries. Similarly in Australia, more women than men reported wanting to participate in work-related training courses but had not participated in any in the last 12 months. A common reason cited was lack of time, presumably often linked to having children.[22] Lack of affordable childcare inhibits women from turning their qualifications into careers — a key explanation for the Paula Principle (see Chapter 5).

Learning at work

So we come back round to the main thrust of the Paula Principle. Why are women working at a level below where their education suggests they could or should be? Is it that men shrug off their relative lack of qualifications, get stuck into building up their skills and competences through training at work, and so manage to shin up career ladders faster than women? If men do more in the way of training at work, it would explain why they continue to earn more and move up the vertical career path more sharply.

This is what I originally expected, but when I looked at the data further, I found that it does not seem to be the case. I was hugely surprised to find that women, on the whole, undertake *more* training at work than men do. I had assumed that, as part of the general picture of female disadvantage at work, they would have fewer opportunities of this kind. Indeed, it was my discovery that this is not the case that sparked the idea of the Paula Principle in the first place. It is, after all, highly telling that women go on adding to their vocational competence at a greater rate than men do, accentuating the educational trends we've seen earlier. Paula is clearly more committed than Peter to learning at work, as well as at school and as an adult generally — and yet ends up with far less to show for it.

It was a full 20 years ago when the participation rates of women in vocational training overtook those of men in the United Kingdom. The gap has grown since then to about three percentage points overall, where it seems to have stabilised. Women in every age group are more likely than men to have taken part in some form of training at work within the last three months — anything from basic health and safety to how to build better teams or get to grips with the latest technology. Three points might not sound much, but when it is 15% against 12% that is a significant difference.[23] As ever, socio-economic status and class is a dominant influence at every level, overshadowing gender effects. Women and men alike with few qualifications take part less in training than their more-qualified colleagues. This is the so-called Matthew effect — to them that hath shall be given. Evidently there is also a Martha effect: better-educated women get much better access to training than less-educated women.

The gender training gap is smallest at jobs with lower educational levels, but even here women take part more often than men. Once we get to graduates, the gap between female and male participation rates widens sharply, to around 10 percentage points or more. For every three highly qualified men who report taking part in training, there are about four women. This does not suggest a lack of commitment to getting on at work.

Social scientist Alan Felstead and his colleagues measured, in a wide variety of workplaces, how far women and men had increased their qualifications and skills at various points between 1992 and 2006. Across a whole range of areas, women's skill levels were shown to have increased at a faster rate.[24] Men still have higher actual skill levels in many areas — but women are catching up. Women are increasingly keen to exercise their skills: in 1992, men rated the opportunity to use abilities and initiative, and access to training, more highly than women; by 2006, the reverse was true.

Iona, Vanessa, and Mandy, the three Geordie women who told their stories earlier, all re-engaged in learning as adults. This was largely through one of the United Kingdom's most successful initiatives in adult education, UnionLearn, in which trade unionists are trained to help their colleagues return to learning. They had all overcome their unsatisfactory school experiences, and were relishing being back in class. A single parent, Mandy worked as a school dinner assistant and as a cleaner — 'like women do' — but she also went back to college to learn maths, English, and book-keeping. She got a job with the local council, moving around in different administrative roles but still studying: 'Whatever the council threw at me, I'd do a course on it — sign language, mental health awareness, welfare rights!' Vanessa is currently doing an IT qualification and looking to do a more advanced diploma afterwards. Her confidence has soared from the learning: 'I've just completed a public speaking course, which is something I never ever thought I could do. I was terrified before doing it, but I really enjoyed it.' While working in a school doing the dinners and holding down cleaning jobs in offices and people's homes, which suited her family responsibilities, Iona also restarted her education, getting three GCSEs. She is now doing a course on leadership and management.

All three women are deeply involved in promoting learning for their colleagues, as UnionLearn representatives. Tellingly, the organisation struggles to engage men in their programmes. Vanessa says: 'We have classes of 12, and it's usually at least 10 women. They want to get on, or into a new occupation. The men are just not interested.' The problem is most acute with the least qualified men.

In sum, over the last decade and a half, women have overtaken men in both aspiration and action to improve their skills at work. They take part more in training, place a higher value on that training, and are keener to find jobs that allow them to use their skills. The gender training gap is remarkably pervasive, existing in almost every occupation, from managerial to routine. It shows up in different degrees in every single region of the United Kingdom. The Celtic fringe goes for the extremes: the gap between the proportions of women and men taking training is largest in Wales (11%), and smallest in Scotland (3.5%).[25] Does it matter what sector people work in? Only in the armed forces and, more surprisingly, the National Health Service does a higher proportion of men than women undertake training. In the private sector, the gap is 3% in favour of women. All in all, it's an impressively comprehensive pattern of greater female acquisition of competences.

So why do women go for training more than men? A stronger, virtuous desire for self-improvement? That's a real option as an explanation: women may well be more conscientious about taking advantage of whatever training opportunities are offered at work, whether these are generous or not. Indeed, this fits with the fact that women are more likely to acknowledge skills deficits — and therefore the need for further training. Men have a greater tendency to think (rightly or wrongly) that they know what they are doing and to resist the idea that they might need to learn something new.[26]

It is also an unfortunate truth that women are more likely to need evidence to prove that they can do a particular job or carry out a particular function. Without the proof, they'll have a harder time convincing bosses that they are indeed competent. They may also want to convince themselves. As Wilma, who works in industry in the West Midlands, said: 'Women *feel* they need the qualifications to compete against their male counterpart.' Other women have recounted how they feel they need to show themselves not just equally but also better qualified in order to compete.

However, there is another important factor that needs to be taken into account in explaining women's higher training activity rates. Almost twice as many women as men work in the public sector, and access to training is consistently more available in the public than the private sector. It outweighs other factors that would tend to depress women's relative access to training, such as working part-time and at lower occupational levels.[27]

Yet the public sector's commendably advanced record on training is potentially double-edged. The economic downturn of the last few years has led to a steep drop in public sector jobs, as well as a very hard squeeze on all forms of expenditure — and training has historically been particularly vulnerable to such squeezes. Thus, even in the public sector, there is likely to be no steady onward march of opportunity.

But there is more to the gender gap in training even than this. Figures tell us only *how many* women and men take part in training. They tell us nothing about *how much* the person actually gets in the way of training: how long it lasts, and how intense it is. An employee engaged in a morning's induction programme may register as having taken part in training, and in the crude figures she will count the same as someone who has enrolled himself in a management course lasting several weeks or even months. The pronouns in the previous sentence are deliberate: where men do take part, they are more likely to have access to longer training courses than women. The higher up you are in the hierarchy, the more likely you are to go on a formal course of some significant duration and, since men are generally higher up the ladder, it follows that they are likely to be favoured in this way. In 2013, in the United Kingdom, about 30% of women undertook training that lasted more than ten hours, compared with 36% of men.[28] So women's comparative advantage in simple participation may be balanced or outweighed by men's relative advantage in the duration of training. Peter's greater intensity to some extent cancels out Paula's more likely engagement.

Whose qualifications count more?

Generations and change

I am going to finish the education side of the story by taking a look down the telescope from the other end, at a set of figures that show not only differences between the sexes but also between different age groups. This gives us a 'life-course' perspective, which should, in my view, be the frame through which we view education of all kinds. We need to look at all the Paula Principle issues across people's lives, extending into retirement and old age, and not only at particular points.

Having no qualifications is not where anyone wants to be. There has, happily, been a decline over decades in the proportions of men and women who are in this position. The graph below starts with the oldest age group — going backwards may have a slightly Benjamin Button feeling of magical rejuvenation, but it gives the right trajectory. Among those aged 60-plus, far more women than men have no qualifications. The expansion of education and raising of the school leaving age in the 1970s in part accounts for the significant drop in unqualified 40- to 49-year-olds, that is, those born roughly between 1960 and 1970. Women have nearly caught up, narrowing a very considerable gap with great speed. They have closed the gap altogether by the time we get to those below 30, and by the next age group there are fewer women than men who have no qualifications. We end up in the youngest age groups with the proportion of unqualified women being a couple of percentage points below that of men.

The generation that grew up in the 1960s and 1970s is nearly the last where far fewer women than men were regularly in some kind of paid employment. The decline is very welcome, though the fact that so many in the oldest age group still have no qualifications is not a cause for national pride. It means that not only did they leave school with no qualifications, but also that they have passed the intervening 40 or more years without managing to acquire a single certificate. Almost all of them will, in the nature of things, have acquired considerable expertise and competences, in and out of the workplace. Much of their skills acquisition will have been in unpaid work, in rearing and managing a family or in voluntary work, and so this is a classic case where it would be a mistake to equate formal qualification with actual skill. Even so, having no qualifications will have been for many women a brake on their career options.

Educational Qualifications (Level 1 or Below/No Qualifications) By Gender, Age, and Percentage of Population in 2006–2008

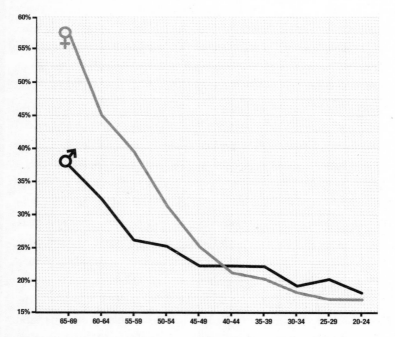

Change in proportions with low or no qualifications. Source: Labour Force Survey.

So where does all this leave us? Quite simply, women as a group continue to build on their initial educational advantage by taking part more in adult education and enjoying better access to training at work. For a long time, women compensated for their lack of formal education by engaging in community forms of adult learning. Now they are strongly present in formal education, too. Personally as well as professionally, they continue to accumulate more human capital than men do. But it doesn't pay off in ways that it should. That's the topic of the next chapter.

3

Competence Under-Rewarded

How women's skills and qualifications
continue to be undervalued

High Wages is the ironic title of a novel by Dorothy Whipple, first published in 1930 (smartly reprinted by Persephone Books in 2009). The heroine, Jane Carter, is a single woman, intelligent but poorly educated, and equipped with few marketable skills. She has no family to support her, and is grateful to get a job in a draper's store, owned by a Mr Chadwick. She and her fellow shopworker, Maggie, are paid a pittance, cheated by Chadwick of commissions they earn on sales and by his wife of the food that forms part of their employment 'package'. They work about 12 hours a day, six days a week.

Although Jane lacks qualifications, she doesn't lack competence. She is also enterprising. She hears that Northgate, a great house on the fringe of the town, is to be turned into a Voluntary Aid Detachment (VAD) hospital, and suggests to Mr Chadwick that he tender to supply the hospital with bed linen, table linen, towels, and so on. Jane takes it on herself to go to Manchester. She returns with a specimen VAD uniform, dresses a wax model in it, and announces outside the shop that such uniforms are supplied within. She procures the blue overalls and veils for the voluntary helpers.

What is the result of her enterprise and skill?

'Mr Chadwick was busier than he had ever been in his life before; money rolled in. Yet he paid Jane one pound a week, and Maggie thirteen and sixpence, and looked with complacency on his wife's schemes to deprive them of their food rations.'[1]

Exploitation — the gap between competence, effort, and reward — has always existed. Today Jane would certainly not lack qualifications, in all likelihood, and she would be far better paid, and better protected (though some of these gains are today far from secure). Yet the reward for her competence would still probably fall some way short of fairness, if not as far as it did in Whipple's novel.

The essence of the Paula Principle is that women do not, in general, reach the levels we would expect when they put their skills and qualifications to work. How can we assess this? It is not straightforward because the Paula Principle involves a double dynamic: the *absolute* progress made by women in getting more education and better jobs, and their progress *relative to men*. They may be doing well on the first of these dimensions, but not nearly so well on the second.

Teasing this out is quite complex. We cannot trace out *career* crossovers between women and men as simply as we have traced *educational* crossovers. In a very broad sense, the working lives of women now have a similar pattern to that of men. They are employed at a similar rate, and many of them work full-time. The average gap between men's and women's starting pay grades is shrinking, at least for professionals. Retirement ages are moving closer together. But, as women get older, their employment *trajectories* — the ups, downs, sideways moves, and interruptions throughout those working lives — continue to diverge considerably from men's, in fact possibly more than before. Seen in that longer 'life-course' frame, women have not caught up to, let alone overtaken, men, whether we look at earnings or at job levels and career patterns. It's from this basic tension that the Paula Principle springs.

Does it make sense to expect career paths to align exactly with educational achievement, so that there is a perfect match between people's qualifications and the job levels they attain? Not much. Even if it were feasible, most of us would not actually want such a strict form of meritocratic bondage.[2] On the other hand, if we think only in terms of literal equality between women and men, we will miss the Paula Principle's double dynamic: women are continually improving their competences, and they are doing so at a rate that is creating an increasing competence gap between them and men. This double dynamic is sending tremors — albeit mild ones, so far — through the structure of our employment systems.

General economic and social progress, and specific measures such as the introduction of the minimum wage, have greatly reduced the kind of gross underpayment that Dorothy Whipple described. But low pay — and I mean truly low pay, where basic living becomes a problem — is still strikingly widespread in rich countries. Women always dominate in these unfortunate ranks. In 2014, most of the 5.3 million employees in the United Kingdom paid below the living wage were women. Twenty-seven per cent of all female employees were paid below the living wage, compared with 16% of males. This simply does not square with their rising levels of competence.

As I've mentioned before, we all know that pay is often not the only reward that people get from work. A sense of satisfaction, of having one's skills properly used, and the social contact it brings — all these count for a lot. So does being able to progress and develop. Being 'valued' is a crucial feature of all this; and arguably for women their actual pay is less directly a measure of value than it is for men. Office cleaners have a host of nitty-gritty problems, low pay and insecurity being major ones, but the issue they cited most often in a recent survey was lack of recognition of the contribution they make to organisations' functioning.[3] Their sense of value was offended. (I'll be dealing with all this in further detail later.)

Pay gaps: the current picture

Two terms that figure prominently in this part of the argument are gap and lag. The *gap* is the *difference in the material rewards* that women and men get from work. The *lag*, by contrast, is the *distance in time* between women getting more education and getting the kind of jobs that adequately reflect this. Understanding lag is crucial for getting a realistic handle on the issue. For example, as more women graduate from medical school, it will take only a few years for this to show up in the proportions of female and male junior doctors, but a good deal more time for it to change the gender balance among senior consultants. Similarly, we can expect more women to graduate as lawyers, but the trudge to become judges will take a lot longer. The same applies to lower-level occupations, as more women aspire to move up the grades in administrative or service jobs. That such lags should occur is natural and inevitable; the question is how long a lag between educational achievement and career attainment is 'reasonable' — not for the individual, but for women as a whole. Pace of change — how fast a goal can realistically be achieved — is often the unstated source of political difference, even when there is agreement on the goal itself.[4] These kinds of changes take time for their effects to be felt, but how long is it reasonable to wait? As American academic and author Carolyn Heilbrun observed, reflecting on a different institution: 'Women have legally transformed the marriage relation in under 150 years: we must ask whether that transformation is not in itself amazing, or whether, on the other hand, it has not, as transformations go, been laggardly.'[5]

Let's take the gap first. Paula's pay is getting closer to Peter's. The UK gender pay gap is slightly worse than the EU average — 79% of the male rate, compared with the European average of 82%, according to Eurobarometer. In the wider international table, Australia sits alongside the United States and the United Kingdom with a gender wage gap slightly above the OECD average.[6] Across these countries, the picture is of progress that is sluggish and inconsistent (see chart below). Although some countries, such as Spain and New Zealand, have narrowed the gap quite considerably between 1986 and 2008, in most others progress has been much slower, and the gap remains 20% or more. Moreover, the picture is not one of sustained progress: although the gender pay gap narrowed between 2000 and 2010, almost all the narrowing happened before 2005. After that, the line gets flatter and flatter. The 2016 Gender Equality Report from the World Economic Forum reaches a sobering conclusion: 'Countries across the world are stalling on economic gender parity, despite many reaching or nearing equality in education.' Apparently, North America is moving backwards. Western Europe, by triumphant contrast, is likely to be the first to close the gap completely — in a mere 47 years ...

Gender Pay Gap — Slow or No Progress

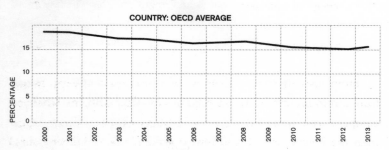

Source: 'Gender Wage Gap', Organisation for Economic Co-operation and Development, http://www.oecd.org/gender/data/genderwagegap.htm, 8 April 2016

In any case, the extent and pace of any convergence depends on exactly who is being compared with whom. Men in general with women in general? Full-timers with full-timers, and part-timers with part-timers? Women and men with the same qualifications? It also depends on whether we look at hourly, weekly, or other rates. These all give us rather different answers. Measuring inequalities is a mind-spinning, multidimensional challenge.[7] Luckily we don't need to dive into this in any detail; all we need is a broad overall idea of the pay gaps between women and men, and of how these have been changing over time.

John Hills' authoritative picture of pay inequality in the United Kingdom shows the results from different ways of measuring the pay gap.[8]

% pay gap

	Hourly wages	Weekly earnings
a) all women versus all men	21	39
b) all women versus full-time men	24	43
c) part-time women versus full-time men	37	71
d) full-time women versus full-time men	13	22

From his painstaking analysis, we can see that the gap ranges from a minimum of 13% to a high of 71%, depending on what you compare with what. (The weekly earnings gaps are always bigger than the hourly ones, because men generally work longer hours.) Even the lowest figure is striking.

We can get a more recent picture, for 2015, from the Office of National Statistics. Their 'headline' figure is just under 10% (9.4% to be exact) in favour of men. This is the gap in the median hourly earnings of full-time employees. In other words, take all men and all women working more than 30 hours a week, sort them into two lists according to their earnings, take the men and the women who are plumb in the middle of that list, and then compare the hourly earnings of these two sets. I've put 'headline' in quotation marks because the 10% was quite widely reported in the United Kingdom as *the* gender pay gap, following common practice. This sadly misrepresents the overall position. If you take *all* employees, that is, part-time as well as full-time, the figure is *over double*, at 19.2%. Since part-timers represent more than a quarter of the workforce, if we have to have a single 'headline' figure, 'all employees' is surely a better benchmark. The figures may be the lowest since the survey began in 1997, but as the Office for National Statistics states, 'the gap has changed relatively little over the last 4 years'.[9]

The figures above hide any number of wrinkles and variations. They do not take people with exactly the same qualifications and compare their pay rates, which is what we would ideally like to see to get a really accurate idea of how the Paula Principle applies. But the simple conclusion is this: women overall match up to or surpass men in their qualifications, yet their pay does not. This is the unmistakable takeaway from these very broad figures.

Occupational segregation: women's pay and the Deep South

One major reason why women are paid less than men is because they work in jobs that are not as highly paid. How obvious can you get? But this apparent tautology disguises a pervasive double segregation.

First there is 'vertical' segregation: if we think of any occupation or organisation as a vertical structure, women are usually found in greater numbers at lower levels. Mr Chadwick and Jane typify this. Supervisors earn more than clerks; corporate managers, more than shop managers; and hospital consultants, more than junior doctors. Women find their way less often from the latter to the former levels. They dominate, if that's the right word, the ranks of the low-paid.

The impact of this is massively increased by ballooning levels of inequality in earnings. In the United Kingdom, the average FTSE

100 CEO's pay in 2014 was 183 times that of the median full-time worker, up from 160 times in 2010. In the United States, the figures are even more extreme: the average pay of the chief executives of America's 327 largest companies is 354 times that of the average US worker — a day's earnings for one equals almost a year's for the other.[10] A different study identifies Australia, along with South Korea, as the country with the highest CEO-to-worker pay inequality.[11] Can anyone seriously rationalise these kinds of disparities as a proportionate reward for superior competence or unusual effort?

Inequality of these dimensions impinges strongly on Paula. The UK-based think tank the High Pay Centre uses the cases of Brenda and Brian — stereotypical, but based on real representative instances — to make the point. Brenda is a qualified nurse who makes £12 an hour, the average wage in the United Kingdom. Brian is a chief executive of one of Britain's biggest companies and receives a £4.3 million pay package. He makes as much in three days as Brenda earns in an entire year. Brian has seen his annual pay increase by £2 million in the last decade, while Brenda's pay has stagnated. He will earn four times as much in one year as she does in her entire lifetime.

The whole scale of income inequality has been almost unimaginably elongated — so much so that it can't even be depicted graphically, for example by stick figures of different sizes alongside one another, because the bottom earners would have to be squashed into invisibility if the top earners were to be fitted in. Almost all of the mega-earners are men. (This, incidentally, distorts some of the figures for the gender gap: most men, as well as most women, get nowhere near such high earnings, but their average incomes look higher as a result.) So the Paula Principle needs to be seen against a backdrop of grotesque financial inequalities that disfigure several Western societies, most notably the United Kingdom and the United States. Thomas Piketty's 2014 blockbuster, *Capital,* has brought this crashing into the public consciousness.[12] The relevance of this to the Paula Principle is stark: although the disproportionate salary packages of a tiny minority exclude and damage the remaining 99% of the population, men and women alike, the impact is indisputably more severe on women.

The second form of segregation is 'horizontal', referring not to the level reached within an occupation but to the *type of occupations* that women and men choose to go into. In a nutshell, finance, engineering, and the private sector generally pay better than care services, teaching, and the public sector, where women are far more frequently to be found.

In part, horizontal segregation reflects subject choices made in school and college, but only up to a point. Even where women choose to study subjects that might seem to open up the way to jobs traditionally dominated by men, they often do not follow this path through to its more lucrative or esteemed higher reaches. To take just one example, more than a third of female physics graduates from the cohort of people born in 1958 went into school teaching, a traditional female occupation. For most, this has depressed their pay (if not their spirit) compared to male physics graduates.

Choosing a lower-paying career path can be a perfectly sensible and satisfactory decision, even if you have other options (see Chapter 8). Women may generally, and wisely, put a higher premium on job satisfaction or work–life balance. Nevertheless, the horizontal segregation of men and women into different occupations carries a powerful material depth charge. Both sexes are worse off in their own segregated areas — that is, men who work in mainly male fields and women who work in mainly female fields, compared with those who work in non-segregated occupations. But it's not symmetrical: the female pay penalty for working in 'feminised' jobs is more severe than the male penalty for working in 'masculinised' jobs.[13] Is this just a coincidence? Hardly. It applies most fiercely at the lower occupational levels — notably the 5Cs of caring, cashiering, clerking, catering, and cleaning, where women figure so heavily — but the same effect has been found for well-qualified graduates, too.[14] So sauces for segregated geese and ganders differ in their degree of tastiness.

The 5Cs: where we find the concentration of low pay.

Switching poultry, we have a chicken-and-egg issue: do occupations that are less well paid just happen to have mainly women working in them, or do occupations become lower paid when more women move into them? Maybe it doesn't matter very much which of the two is more often the case. The latter certainly happens to some extent, even in quite a well-paid field such as medicine. If the feminisation of an occupation is linked to its having lower pay rates (not necessarily in absolute terms, but relative to what they would have been if men dominated the occupation), this sits very uncomfortably with the fact that the skill levels of the women working in it are likely to be rising (both absolutely, and relative to men). On any count, there's something odd happening when we find women increasing their qualifications, using those qualifications to enter job areas where they had not previously figured much — and then finding that those jobs do not reward them as well as they rewarded their male predecessors.

Lags: the pace of pay convergence

There has certainly been progress towards eliminating unreasonable pay gaps between men and women, yet it happens at such a slow pace that it needs a fairly expert snailtracker to detect it. A 2016 report from the Chartered Management Institute showed that a female manager would have to work for at least 14 years beyond her pensionable age of 65 to earn the same amount of money as a male counterpart.[15] At this rate, women will wait another 57 years before actually achieving equality of pay; since we are already more than 40 years on from the passing of the Equality Act in the United Kingdom and Australia, and more than 50 years on from the passing of the Equal Pay Act in the United States, this means a full century of catch-up time.

Researchers Kate Purcell and Peter Elias have been tracking all UK graduates who completed their university degree in 1995, seeing what happened to them as they moved into jobs. When they first enter the job market, women are more likely to land non-graduate jobs, and to take longer to get into the graduate jobs. We then find divergence, not convergence, as the graduates move further into their careers. In their first job after graduation, the average earnings gap between men and women was 11%. Two years later, in 1997–98, this had grown to 15%, and by 2002–3, to 19%.[16] The widening gap reflects occupational choice, with men choosing more lucrative areas to work in, but it also reflects motivation or readiness to negotiate higher salary levels. Men find it easier to argue assertively on their own behalf — something we will come back to in Chapter 6.

Now here comes a set of figures that I think are really important. They are about the way the gender pay gap changes *across age groups*. They are for full-timers only (yes, I'm sinning against what I said earlier about looking at all workers, but it's forced on me — the part-time figures are not there). For those aged 22 to 29, the gap is 6%. This rises to 8% for 30- to 39-year-olds. And then, for 40- to 49-year-olds, it triples to 23%; for 50- to 59-year-olds, it goes up again, to 24%; and for those 60 and over, it drops just a little, to 21%.[17] These figures relate to the UK context, but patterns are similar for other developed countries, such as Australia.[18]

That's a pretty dramatic profile of a cliff edge in mid-life. Some of it is because the current generation of older women have fewer qualifications. But as we know from seeing how women have leapt forward educationally, the 40- to 49-ers will already have caught up with men in terms of qualifications. The key question in relation to the Paula Principle is whether we will see the age profile of the gender pay gap change significantly, as the wave of qualifications rolls along, sweeping this generation of older women also to have higher competence levels than men. Already now there is little intrinsic reason for this tripling of the gap after age 40; as the years go on, it will likely become even starker an anomaly, unless something changes.

Women and men's chances of getting jobs at all, or good jobs, or promotions, are quite strongly influenced by the historical point when they were born.[19] This makes comparisons tricky, but help is at hand. We have some wonderful information from UK studies that have tracked thousands of people — 'cohorts', in the jargon — over many years, from the moment they were born, or even before. It's not that those studied have been constantly monitored by some Big Brother–like chip implant, but they have been interviewed every five years or so to see what has been happening in their personal and professional lives. This gives us truly powerful insights into their careers and lets us flesh out this pay gap over the generations more fully.

From the three national cohort studies of people who were born in 1946, 1958, and 1970, and who have been followed to their current ages — 70s, late 50s, and late 40s respectively — we can draw the following broad conclusions.

- There has been an *overall decrease in the gender pay gap* experienced by women in the three different cohorts. For those born in 1946 (mostly now retired), women's median hourly pay was about 60% of men's; for the 1970 cohort (today in their middle-to-late working lives), the ratio is closer to 80%. In other words, this very broad-brush picture shows a degree of convergence between male and female pay rates, comparing like with like.
- This sounds like healthy progress, but the convergence should not obscure the *unequal treatment that persists*. Women are paid less than men with similar qualifications and similar backgrounds. For the youngest cohort, the gap was about 10–12% in 2004, when they were 34. Some of this is because women go into different occupations from men, and these generally pay less, as we have observed. But this does not account for more than a fraction of the gap.
- Now for the curves. Look at the graph on page 59, which shows how the pay gap starts at different points but expands over time. It's a very simple figure, but it contains some implications that fundamentally challenge any complacency about simple progress. First, although *the pay gap has decreased very significantly between the two generations, the gap widens over time, as each generation gets further into its career path.*
- In addition, and crucially, *this happens at a faster rate for the younger generation*. So for those born in 1970, the gap at age 26 was only just over 10%, compared with nearly double that for the 1958 cohort measured at roughly the same age (23 years old).

This is the kind of progress one would expect, especially given that the women in the younger generation had begun to pull ahead of the men of their age in terms of qualifications. But for this same younger generation, by age 34, the earnings gap had increased by eight points to 18.5%; at a similar age in the previous generation the gap had also increased, but it had gone up only about four percentage points, from 19.5% to 23.4%. The figure shows how the gap starts smaller, but then *widens at a faster rate* for the younger generation. And yet these are the women who have a larger qualification advantage over the men in their cohort than did their 1958 sisters.

- In short, the pay gap has declined across the generations — but it grows right back over time.

How the Gap Grows as Generations Age

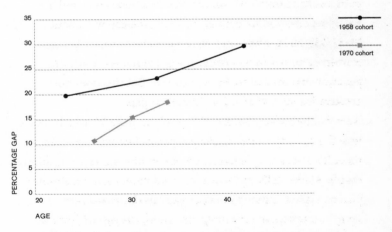

Percentage differences in average hourly wages between women and men at different ages and in two cohorts, born in 1958 and 1970. They are adjusted for differences in school ability, educational attainment, years of work experience, and years in current job. Source: researcher Dr Jenny Neuburger. I am grateful to Jenny for this data and chart, which are from her doctoral research.

I've dwelt on the trajectories over time for a particular reason. Some might say that the Paula Principle really applies only to less educated women. Highly educated women can and do make it to the top professional levels. British economist Alison Wolf, an acknowledged expert in the interface between education and the labour market, argues that such women now have little in common with the rest of their gender.[20] Does the Paula Principle apply only to the 70% of women who are outside this elite? Even if so restricted, it would still be important. But launching into a career is one thing; maintaining the upward trajectory over decades is quite another, as we have seen. That's why we need to see how far even the elite, educated women sustain the parity they have achieved in the early stages of their careers. While I have already agreed that class trumps gender, I'm not convinced that even stellar educational success protects high-flyers from the Paula Principle. They may just be likely to feel its effects later than other women.

Until we have followed the younger women and men through to later periods of their life, we cannot fully know what change has occurred from one generation to the next. Information on this should be available fairly soon — though, of course, by then another generation or two will have come over the horizon, and we'll have to start the analysis over again ...

South Korea: a strong case of the Paula Principle

South Korea provides an unusually powerful illustration of how education can do a lot to change societies, and the place of women within them — but can't do it all. The country has gone through a massive economic and educational transformation in the last decades. In the 1950s, a large proportion of Korean children received no formal education at all. Over the last quarter of the 20th century, South Korea hauled itself from near the bottom of the OECD educational league table to very close to the top, at least as measured by school achievement. The upwards surge involved massive public investment and huge private effort: the Korean catchphrase 'four hours bad, five hours good' referred to the desirable amount of studying undertaken additional to school time — *per day*. Industrialisation and technological progress carried on in a rapid dynamic interaction.

In education, South Korean girls have made particularly fast progress. Their reading scores at age 15 outstrip boys by 35 points. They are among the most educated young women in the world.[21] Their enrolment rate in higher education is extraordinary, at over 82%. More than half of them have completed a college education.

Moreover, when it comes to choice of vocational training, they are not confined to traditional subjects. Twenty-nine per cent of South Korean women in vocational secondary training are in engineering, construction, or manufacturing, compared with an OECD average of 7%.[22] So it's not at all the case that the women are succeeding primarily in the kinds of arts subjects traditionally associated with women.

But the success stops short at the gates of the workplace. South Korea has the biggest wage gap of all OECD countries, at 39%. Fewer than half of South Korean women are in work. Almost uniquely, university-educated women are actually less likely to work than their less-educated sisters. There are only 8.1 women managers for every 100 male managers, while the OECD average is close to 30%. Social attitudes reflect this: along with the Polish, South Koreans are most likely to think that men should be given priority in employment.[23]

In short, the Korean case is a particularly strong instance of the Paula Principle: a very rapid educational crossover co-existing with a persistent high differential in earnings and careers. It's a country to watch for how this blockage at work interacts with social practices and attitudes: will the surge in women's human capital be powerful enough to drive change elsewhere? What we can say for now is that South Korea illustrates just how much the effects of educational progress can be blunted by the values and habits in other parts of society — the workplace and the home.

Part time, full time

Crucially, the figures I have given paint only a very partial picture because they refer to full-time pay. I've already said that most discussions of employment commonly focus on full-time work and therefore marginalise part-timers. The way that statistics are constructed does the same. But, now, numerically the balance between full-timers and part-timers is shifting, having been given a rude further shove by the recession that followed the global financial crisis of 2007–8. Between 2008 and 2012, full-time employment in the United Kingdom fell by nearly 700,000, while part-time employment rose by 400,000. Full-time employment has partially recovered, but part-timers now number over eight million, and make up more than 27% of the total workforce.[24] Thirty-eight per cent of employed women work part-time in the United Kingdom, and an identical proportion in Australia, well above the OECD average of 26%.[25]

Scarlet Harris from the Trades Union Congress puts it this way: 'Stereotypes really kick in for part-timers, about them not being as committed to the job. They are often not considered for training or promotion. The irony is that they often give full-time value for part-time wages.' She sees the part-time issue as primarily one of job design, that is, organising work so that it can be done on a flexible schedule. 'There simply are not enough quality jobs advertised on a part-time basis. The reality is that if you're going out there looking for a part-time job, it means a huge drop in pay, and in your prospects. Yet there are just a handful of jobs where working part-time is a genuine problem — shipping, for example. There are very few areas where it's genuinely impossible.'

– i HAVE AMBITION, IS THAT ABNORMAL ?

Of course, some part-timers do well. Predictably, those in managerial and professional jobs can earn quite reasonable amounts, especially if they are able to combine several sources of income, such as non-executive directorships. But the bulk of part-timers are poorly paid, many of them very poorly. Their chances of progressing upwards are very much smaller, simply because they work part-time. The gap between different work statuses is well captured by an example of the irregular verbs made famous by Bernard, the soothing civil servant in the TV series *Yes Minister*. In one episode, Bernard smoothly sums up the hierarchy of work statuses thus: 'I have a portfolio career. You work flexibly. He or (usually) she is a part-timer.'[26] It is indeed usually a she.

By being better educated, women and men bring many additional advantages to their communities and their societies, as well as to their children (if they have any). That's why taxpayers still support public investment in education, including in higher education, where the private gains are considerable.

For, of course, work itself is not all about money, or even kudos. Carol Shield's wonderful *The Stone Diaries* traces the story of Daisy Flett, née Goodwill, who is born near the start of the 20th century and lives into the 1990s. The story is told obliquely, through many eyes. Daisy does not have much of a career as such. After her husband dies, she begins to write a weekly gardening column (as Mrs Green Thumb) for the local Ottawa paper, *The Recorder*. It's barely paid at all — about as peripheral a position as you can get — but the column flourishes, and it nourishes her. Then disaster falls; she is replaced by an insider. We hear about it via a letter from the insider himself:

Dear Mrs Flett
I've read your letter carefully and I can assure you I under-
stand your feelings. But I believe Jay explained the paper's
policy to you, that full-time staffers have first choice of
columns. As you well know, I've been filling in with the
gardening column from time to time, all those times you've
been away, and, to tell you the honest truth, I've had quite

a lot of appreciative letters from readers who especially like
the fact that my columns are illustrated and take the male
point of view … Think of it this way: our readers are always
changing, and so must we. After nine years of being Mrs
Green Thumb, I feel sure that you too will welcome a change.
With best wishes
James (Pinky) Fulham

But Daisy does not welcome the change at all: 'The spring and summer of 1965 — those were terrible months for Mrs Flett, as she slid day by day along a trajectory that began in resignation, then hardened into silence, then leapt to a bitter and blaming estrangement from those around her …'[27]

We learn that different characters in the book have different explanations for the decline, but it is brutally clear that it is the loss of her job that has caused it. (It is made worse by the fact that 'Pinky' Fulham knew Daisy personally and had come close to taking their friendship further, so he is being more than a tad disingenuous in the way he writes to her.) Putting her gardening expertise to use had fulfilled her and gained her recognition. Now that is gone. *Recorder* readers have lost a treasured columnist, and Daisy has lost a big part of her life.

Part-time does not mean insignificant. The meaning of work goes well beyond the money it brings. Maggie Tulliver might have been keen to accumulate more than her five shillings, and Jane Carter definitely needed a better reward. But the Paula Principle is about how far women are able to put their competences to work, and the financial reward is only one component. Many women want their commitment to work to be properly recognised, and to have some sense of progression in what they do. You could say that these two components — recognition and progression — are what combine to make a 'career', even though that may not be the conventional meaning of the word. The question is, who does the recognising, and who decides on the progress?

We met Mandy from the North East in the previous chapter. When she went back into employment, she worked as a customer service officer in welfare rights, answering queries from people about their entitlements to benefits and support services. She was committed to the work, and did much more than her job formally required: designing leaflets, helping her organisation to get Investors in People and Best Value status (widely recognised best practice standards in the United Kingdom), designing training materials, and monitoring the performance of the service. 'But I wasn't being paid for that kind of job,' she notes. 'I just got paid as the lady who answered the telephone.'

Mandy told her manager that she wanted to become a welfare rights officer, but he said she was too good at doing what she was doing and he didn't want her to move on. He got two more girls in — whom Mandy trained and supported. In time, she was given a pay increase, but only by taking another job, in the management information team. 'Yes, it was more money, but I wanted to work with people and in welfare rights,' she says. Eventually she moved jobs again, becoming a disability housing support officer.

Mandy is determined to go on learning. She thinks maybe she will do an Open University course in employment law, and will look for jobs in human resources, since she knows that her current job will be disappearing. She's not at all sure she'll be able to progress. The council won't offer her a management post because of her union activity.

Careers can begin at any time. Iona was another of our North East trio. After she restarted her education, getting three GCSEs (basic grade qualifications), this was enough to prompt her to apply for a job in a hospital operating theatre; she didn't get it, but was later offered a job without having to go for another interview. 'So that was the start of my National Health Service career. I realised that "career" didn't just mean being a doctor or a solicitor. I realised I wasn't too old and, if I started taking these things like a diploma on, people wouldn't think I was foolish.'

Yet it's not easy to move up. Iona works as a phlebotomist but, despite its impressive name, this is a low-grade job. 'I'm a Band 2 worker in the NHS, a low-paid woman worker. When I took on the role as a UnionLearn rep, I didn't know how to use computers, didn't know how to do roadshows, didn't have a clue how to talk about the value of lifelong learning, how to talk to employers about the value of supporting their staff to learn, how to do presentations — if someone had told me I'd have been capable of doing this, I would have burst out laughing.' She is deeply grateful to her trade union for its support. She is also grateful to her employer for allowing her time off to do the courses. But it has not yet led to a promotion. She has no regrets about all the efforts she has put into her learning: 'It's been a fantastic opportunity. But whether I'll get a job on the strength of it and all that I've learned, I don't know.'

Clearly, graduates are not the only ones with 'careers'. Iona definitely thinks of herself as having one. It's just as important for someone with relatively few qualifications to have a fair chance of moving up a grade or two. In fact, it's arguably more important, since they are likely to be poorer and the jobs they are in are likely to be less agreeable than those that graduates start in — or used to. The cohort studies enable researchers to look at what happens to a broad range of people who start out in a low-paid, low-quality job (which these days includes quite a few graduates). They find that men generally manage to get themselves out of these jobs. For most of them, the low-grade job is 'a stepping stone rather than a trap', and can often be seen as a period of experimentation or even an investment in gaining wider experience. Women also move up, but with two crucial differences: they are more likely to slip downwards again to their initial low grade;

and their jumps upwards are shorter, often only to the second-lowest grade.[28] These are hugely different career trajectories, especially in an era when so much is made of social mobility.

Finding images that fit: metaphors for women at work

Figures can be extremely dry. Is there another way to get a grasp on such trajectories and what they mean for the Paula Principle? Imagination will help here. Analogies and metaphors can illuminate complex issues in ways that literal accounts do not. They are embedded in our daily life and language, and so shape our ways of thinking.[29] For instance, the 'glass ceiling' is such a vivid image for how we think about blocks to women's careers that it has been in common parlance ever since the *Wall Street Journal* article that launched it in 1986.

It has also generated several vitrinal variants. The 'glass escalator' speeds men up to the more rarified levels of feminised occupations, sliding them smoothly above the women crowded below, whom they then command. The 'glass cliff', by contrast, is a fatally slippery surface down which women slide if they make a single mistake.[30] The 'glass wall' partitions women from men, often excluding them from opportunity or career-helpful conversation.[31] I'm sure there are other riffs on the glass theme out there.

But there is a downside to such a striking image. When I talk about the Paula Principle, I have found that people grasp the principle very quickly — but also that in most cases their thoughts flick straight to the higher levels of career professionals: why so few women become CEOs, judges, or Members of Parliament. This is understandable, since these are the inequalities that are much better researched and publicised, and they are the positions of power that affect us all. 'Ah, so you're looking at the glass ceiling,' they say, and so I am — in part.

But, as I hope I've shown, the Paula Principle does not apply only to women's difficulty in getting to the top of organisations, which is where the glass ceiling is usually located. It applies to all levels of organisation and occupation; it is as much — in fact, more — about the clerk who does not become a supervisor as it is about a vice-president who does not make it to the very top. The Paula Principle applies in different ways to these different groups. So the glass ceiling doesn't quite cut it, so to speak.

This is the view that Alice Eagly and Linda Carli put forward compellingly in their book *Through the Labyrinth*.[32] They argue that the glass-ceiling image implies an absolute and invisible barrier that exists at an atypically high organisational level, and it diverts attention away from the barriers that exist at entry level. The absence of women at board level reflects a large-scale and continuous filtering out of women as people move up the organisational ladder. The remarkable solitariness of the single woman among, say, a board with 20 members can be traced back to thousands fewer women than men making progress at far lower grades — less newsworthy maybe, but fundamental to the process that produces the glaring imbalance further up. Concentrating our gaze only on the top storeys has quite significant consequences for how the whole issue of women's success is conceptualised.

So the glass-ceiling metaphor can skew the argument badly. 'It makes me feel like all this is nothing to do with me,' is a fairly typical remark from women who do not see themselves as top leaders, but who nonetheless have an interest in making progress at work. Eagly and Carli propose the labyrinth as an alternative image: a place where women of many different types set foot, sometimes quite cheerfully but sometimes in what quickly becomes confused distress, seeking one of the variety of openings that might allow them to get further on.

Finding a way through the labyrinth

Labyrinths, though, are usually artfully created. They tend to have only one or two entry and exit points. Labyrinths at work tend to be much less tidy, and have a greater number of disguised passages. There may also be more than just one Minotaur waiting to make a meal of any woman who is too persistent in seeking her way through.

Perhaps we could try starting at the other end? 'Sticky floor' has been used to describe women's difficulty getting started on a promotion path. For various reasons, it's hard for them to prise their feet off the floor. The glue on the floor is not as strong and unyielding as the glass ceiling: women may be able to wrench their feet free without having to smash anything. But sticky floors sap the energy and make the going harder. The floors are at every level, from basement to just beneath the penthouse suite.

A sticky patch?

As an image, the sticky floor gets closer than the glass ceiling to evoking the frustrations of those whose competences are under-recognised. It has a much wider application, as Scarlet Harris from the Trades Union Congress emphasises: 'We've always said it's not really about the glass ceiling, it's the sticky floor. We're always getting asked for our views about getting women onto boards, but this is so far removed from what matters to most women. It's a tiny, tiny minority.'

In any case, most organisations are not tidy vertical structures, and most careers are not spent within a single organisation. As one friend drily observed: 'Women climb the ladder, and when they get to the top they find it was leaning on the wrong wall!'

I think of the typical organisation as more like a ziggurat — one of those sprawling Mesopotamian structures with huge bases and successively smaller and irregular tiers. Smashing through a ceiling might not open up the route to the top, but only to a dead-end lower level.

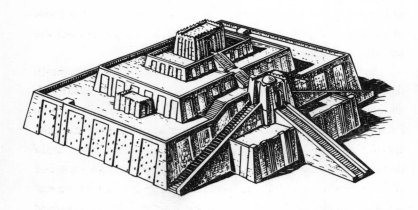

Negotiating the ziggurat

Or we could visualise the typical career trajectory of women as similar in effect to a leaky pipe — a powerful and evocative image of wastefulness. The strong flow of qualified women in the early stages of a career in any given occupation dwindles to a tiny drip at the far end. The metaphor has been applied with striking effect to scientific careers where the various stages of career progression can be quite easily defined, and where the declining numbers of women at each stage are readily seen. As the Royal Society reported in 2010: 'Women are still under-represented in the latter stages of scientific careers, particularly in the physical sciences. While 35% of all researchers in science-related disciplines are women, the proportion falls to 30% for lecturers, 21% for senior lecturers and just 11% for professors.'[33]

It's also worth asking where the leaks leak to. If physics graduates go into teaching, this is much less of a loss to our scientific base than if they give up their subject entirely. Even if they do move into a completely different field, it could well be argued that the wider irrigation of scientifically qualified people into other fields is useful fertilisation. But it remains the case that most are lost to science, and, more generally, that there is a huge leakage of more-or-less specialised talent. Inadequate career flexibility and low levels of management awareness and support mean that the leakages are wasteful, not fruitful.

The pipe image is close to a much more familiar one: the brain drain. This usually refers to the loss of one country's talents through emigration, but it gains a fresh meaning in the context of the Paula Principle. The Equal Opportunities Commission has given it a quite specific and, I think, telling application: the 'hidden brain drain' occurs as competent women move to part-time employment and slither down the occupational ladder to a lower grade. This is a real waste of talent from which no one gains (unlike in the standard version of a brain drain, where at least the receiving country benefits).

I'd like to add one more image to the pot: that of the mosaic. In Chapter 9, I argue that the key way out of the Paula Principle is for more men to abandon the relentless full-time, vertical career path, and at some point work off-schedule, as it were, by going part-time, or taking time out for personal development, for family, or for other reasons. Men should be able to fit these pieces together without being regarded as if they had just thrown in the career towel. My conclusion — maybe unsurprisingly, in a book by a man about women — is that more women will be able to fulfil their potential at work only if more men change their attitudes to employment and pursue mosaic careers. I call this 'reverse convergence'. Up until now, women and men have been converging in their employment patterns — but the convergence has been almost all one way, by women moving towards male patterns. The time has come for a reciprocal movement by men towards patterns that are traditionally regarded as 'female'.[34]

Reverse convergence will not lead to total symmetry, with equal proportions of men and women working non-traditional patterns at each point in their lifetime careers. There will still be more housewives than househusbands (though we could probably junk both terms). But there is huge scope for a move to a more balanced distribution, so that women are doing less of the second shift, and men are thinking more about how they divide their time between work and other activities. Of course, this is already happening in many places, but it's often by default rather than as a matter of positive choice. Reverse convergence means more men actively choosing to move towards those non-traditional patterns, without giving up their commitment to work. It's the essential corollary to the educational crossover.

I doubt if there is a perfect metaphor to match the many different aspects of the Paula Principle. Yet the use of such images as a way of exploring complex issues is often rich and fruitful, opening up new ways of conceiving them. Metaphors shake up our thinking and generate new insights.

Finding images that fit is an integral part of the Paula Principle. It's very clear that a substantial number of women now launch themselves into the jobs market on more or less equal terms with men. For some, the trajectory will carry on this way, while others will find themselves falling behind. This will happen at various points — most usually around childbirth, but at other times, too. So it's crucial that we can conceive an image, or set of images, flexible enough to cover high-flyers, late bloomers, and those who simply want their just desserts, in the sense of having their growing set of competences properly recognised.

But perhaps that's enough metaphors for now. In this chapter we've seen how gaps persist in the rewards women and men receive from work, in both wages and careers, over the lifecourse. Some of this is because women's employment is concentrated in occupations that are lower paid — but we've also asked the question whether such occupations are lower paid because it is mainly women who work in them. Higher-status professions where women are now coming to outnumber men may be seeing their rewards drop. Above all, though, I've argued that the division into 'full-time' and 'part-time' employment is damaging to women's career prospects. We need to reframe the discussion, with a different set of images for what we think of as 'careers'.

4

Explaining the Paula Principle

Factor one — discrimination and values

Why is it that working women tend to stay at a level below their true competence? Whenever I ask this question, I find that people, female or male, need no prompting to respond. Often they have a story from their own experience, professional or personal. But that doesn't really account for how far the Paula Principle extends, why it continues to operate, and how much it matters — to women and to society more generally.

The five-factor approach

There are five angles, which I call the PP factors, that seem to me most salient in explaining the Paula Principle. The first four are *discrimination and values, caring responsibilities, self-confidence and identity,* and *social capital.* These all represent barriers that, in an ideal world, shouldn't exist, as they all point to practices that go against what is fair, and economically and socially beneficial. In Chapter 8, I discuss another explanation for why women do not rise to the levels we might expect: PP factor five, *choice.* This is a positive rather than a negative factor, because Paula is making an active decision not to go further up the career ladder. As we shall see, it takes us in a rather different direction.

Since setting up a website in 2012 to explore the Paula Principle further, I have been asking the visitors to the site to state which of the five factors they think is most explanatory. The diagram below represents votes cast to date; limited as it is, at least it shows all the factors overlapping and interacting.

The PP Factors: votes on their importance

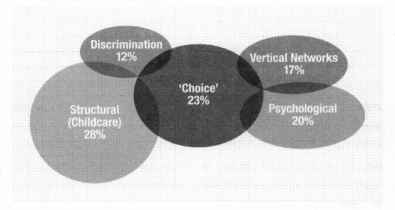

This figure broadly represents the votes cast between 2012 and 2016 on the website, with some additional results from groups I polled face to face. Visitors to the site were asked to pick one factor only. However, as the figure shows, the factors are not separate but interact. Source: http://www.paulaprinciple.com

In discussing the Paula Principle with various groups, I've sometimes since awarded each member of the group 20 votes to allocate among the various factors. They can, if they choose, allocate all 20 votes to one factor, or split them up. For example, if someone thinks that it's all about self-confidence, with just a dash of discrimination, they might give 15 votes to PP factor three and five votes to PP factor one. The pattern is broadly the same as that in the figure above. The five-factor approach lets people express different perceptions of what they think explains the Paula Principle. It also throws light on differences in values and preferences — that is, on what people think *should* be happening. It's obvious, for example, that different factors will carry different weight in different countries. Few of us would judge discrimination, as a factor, to be as strong in egalitarian Sweden as it is in a reactionary state such as Saudi Arabia.[1] But it's also the case that people from the same country and same culture will disagree in their views on what gender fairness means, and on how high a priority it should be given. Swedes are not uniform gender egalitarians, and some deviant Saudi men might favour fair employment opportunities for women.

It isn't only country but also generation, class, and occupation that will have a bearing on people's views. Kirsten, whom we met in Chapter 1, had been the sole engineering graduate in a class of 150 and went into the oil industry. Naturally, her experience was radically different from that of the women we'll meet in the next chapter, who have jobs in health or education within their highly feminised workforces (which is not to say that workforces with female majorities are automatically women-friendly).

Organisations within a particular sector may offer different profiles — not all oil companies are the same in how they encourage or discourage women in their careers, nor are all primary schools. When it comes to action, for example to reduce the segregation of women and men into different kinds of job, it seems to me sensible to have targets that take account of the organisation or occupation as it currently is: attaining 20% as the proportion of women in engineering or men in childcare would represent a highly significant shift from the current state of play and so might be a reasonable target for those sectors, even though it's well below the average for all occupations. However, not everyone agrees on this; some argue for a universal threshold across all occupations. Some argue for an exact 50/50 divide between men and women as the universal ideal. This seems to me to be a wrong-headed obeisance to numerical equality, primarily because it treats women and men as two wholly discrete groups, which are, by implication, usually opposing each other. It also excludes all those who do not identify with a specific gender, now emerging as a significant if small minority.

The five-factor approach throws up interesting differences in how people respond, especially those with different levels of education. The results are not always predictable. You might think, for example, that success generates self-confidence (PP factor three), and so it does; but Brenda, a high-flying civil servant who has been successful by anyone's standards, told me that even after she had reached her previous, very senior, grade and done the job well, she still needed personal encouragement to believe that she could go yet one step further (which she did, and successfully, too). We can't predict how the different factors will play out just by looking at how well people have done so far.

Finally, the approach can help us explore differences of value and perception even within small groups such as families. Imagine members of the same household — mothers, daughters, sons, fathers, great-aunts — casting their votes on the factors that explain career trajectories. The odds are that they will give very different answers, with some definite risk of domestic conflagration. Age is one of the things that will influence this: an older women's experience of discrimination (against themselves, and against others) will be markedly different from that of their daughters and granddaughters, and I would expect each generation often to score the factors differently. Exploring these variations is what makes the Paula Principle a fascinating but also, I hope, useful notion.

Discrimination and differences in values

'I never experienced discrimination. When you're in a female minority and you're quite good, then if anything it's to your advantage.

If anything, I was nurtured — no, just hearing myself say that, it's totally the wrong word — I was *promoted*. Definitely never any discrimination.'

Nuala is a political journalist who enjoys a varied and successful career. She has been a deeply involved political press secretary, held a position in national newspaper journalism, and now works in digital publishing, on current affairs. Her statement above is, you would think, unambiguous. But she went straight on to describe her reaction when she found out that she had been paid less than male counterparts. 'This thing about being underpaid: as a woman you can think everything's fine, and then you find out you're being paid 20%, 50% less than someone else. I just felt horrified, appalled, hurt, wounded — it's not to do with the money, it's to do with value: you feel, *I'm undervalued*.

'You can have a really great time working in politics, but when you get into the hierarchy it's a whole different matter. I had a great time working behind the scenes in politics, really enjoyed it, and then I discovered that I was being significantly underpaid. The justification for it was that the job I was doing didn't involve managing other people, but I felt very hard done by.'

Here is a highly intelligent, politically aware woman who first tells me quite emphatically that she has never experienced discrimination, and in the next breath goes on to say how hurt she was to discover that she was being paid significantly less than men doing similar work. This happened not only in her role as a political press secretary but also as a financial journalist, when both she and other women were underpaid relative to male colleagues. In the latter post, it took the arrival of a female managing director to uncover and resolve the issue. 'She came round and said, "We've been looking at the spreadsheets and it turns out you should have been being paid more than you have been,"' Nuala recalled, with a slightly ambiguous laugh.

This tells us a lot about differences in the way discrimination is perceived, and how people define it in highly contrasting ways. It also prompts some significant questions about attitudes to value, and to how value is related to financial reward. Discrimination, PP factor one, accounted for 18% of website votes, but not everyone defines discrimination in the same way.

Initially, Nuala seemed to be simply contradicting herself: first she says she has never experienced discrimination, then immediately tells me that she has been underpaid. But it is not as simple as that. The key, it seems to me, is in her attitude towards reward: the money was not at all irrelevant, but in front field was professional recognition. She had not felt discrimination in respect of her ability to do interesting and rewarding work, and this was what counted. As long as she felt that her work was valuable, in the double literal sense of able to be valued and actually accorded value, the pay was a background issue. But when the discrepancy emerged, the impact was huge *because it undermined this sense of being valued*. I don't have the sense that after the discovery Nuala actually felt any more insecure about the intrinsic quality of her work — she had enough self-confidence to resist that — but the discrimination opened up a *gap that had not previously existed between value and reward*. The result was, 'I felt really hurt because I'd been absolutely … [it was like] "Oh, thanks a lot, you guys."' Nuala learnt her lesson; her life partner is a business coach and, for her current job in digital journalism, he coached her on how to negotiate an appropriate pay level.

At other times, discrimination is felt more directly. Flora is also a journalist, now a recognised foreign correspondent at a national daily newspaper. Previously she worked for an international press agency. She has been aware of discrimination from quite an early stage in her career. In the agency, she tried several times for a pay rise, and was always fobbed off. Then she discovered that her colleagues were all being paid more. She sent an email to her employers — essentially exactly the same as the previous ones: 'I just added the sentence: "I understand I'm being paid less than my colleagues — most of whom are men." My memory is that I got a memo back within half an hour — it may not have been quite that, but it was certainly very rapid. I didn't even mention legal action. I had a 15% pay rise almost immediately. Of course, I was happy, but it shouldn't have taken that.'

Flora may have been able to stand up for herself, but she also aimed to promote other women's interests. 'When I worked at [the agency], I ran an unofficial women's union. I told all the women journalists what I was paid and what I'd been paid at different points in my career, and I encouraged them to share that information as well.'

Women are still regularly passed over for appointments or promotion on grounds that have nothing to do with their abilities and everything to do with their sex. (Of course, women also sometimes get jobs because of their sex, but not in the same systemic way.) These days, the negative discrimination is more likely to be covert or even subconscious, rather than overt. One important aspect of covert discrimination is the tendency, as we have discussed, for women to be channelled into educational pathways that lead to lower-paying occupations, or away from higher-paying ones. So for Paula it's hairdressing, teaching, or the health service, while Peter gets stuck into finance or engineering.

Discrimination as a word incorporates an odd ambivalence. In one sense, it implies a capacity to tell the difference between things, aesthetically or technically. It's pretty useful to be able to discriminate between different colours (notably at traffic lights, which men are less able to do than women), or between flat and sharp if, like me, you struggle to play an instrument with even minimal musicality. But discrimination has its dark side, and bears down heavily on those who suffer its consequences. To discriminate in this sense is to differentiate unreasonably, and it's usually done by people with power to people without power.

One difficulty in judging whether or not there is discrimination, and if so how serious it is, is that what counts as unreasonable is always changing as social habits and expectations evolve. Therefore, what constitutes discrimination will often be a matter of dispute. Are young people unreasonably discriminated against by a voting age of 18? If doctors refused to give my 98-year-old mother a new heart, would they be discriminating against her? Do 'normal-sized' aeroplane seats discriminate against obese passengers — or against these passengers' compressed neighbours? The contours are always shifting, and certainly so in relation to what counts as sex discrimination.

Sex discrimination has been illegal in the United Kingdom, the United States, and Australia for upwards of 40 years. In the past, though, direct discrimination has been openly sanctioned by law, as when the marriage bar forced female teachers or public servants in the United Kingdom to resign if they got married. As a result, women had to choose, I imagine often painfully, between teaching children and having them, between a career and a partner. How many competent women were, over the decades, ruled out of careers where they would have made a fine contribution? Surely it runs to millions, though we cannot know, since most of those affected had little opportunity to register their feelings about it.[2]

Formal and overt discrimination of that kind is more rare today, although it certainly still exists. Important here is the way the effect of discrimination persists over time, so that the cumulative impact affects a whole career. This, of course, is particularly relevant to older generations. One contributor to the Paula Principle website said:

This subject is a painful one for me, Tom — as I suspect it is for many women of my generation (I am 64). We entered a male-dominated workplace in our 20s, at a time when women were condescended to in private as well as professional relationships.

In a long career in the print media, I have been shocked repeatedly by prejudice against women; it takes great strength as well as practical resources to withstand this ... I believe the fundamental [PP] factor is discrimination.

Even in institutions that one might expect to be sensitive to the issue, glaring examples of discrimination occur on pay and promotion. Universities' commitment to reason doesn't always extend to rewarding women and men reasonably. Liz Schafer had an exhausting four-year struggle to win compensation over a gender pay gap of around £9,000 between herself and comparable professors — not an isolated instance.[3] A similar, if less gruelling, episode was described by another visitor to the website, who worked in academia:

I have kept three letters from the director of human resources from when I was elected dean, each one apologising for getting my honorarium/salary wrong. Fortunately I had a male fellow non-professorial dean who was willing to tell me what he was getting. Firstly he was actually getting a bigger honorarium (second letter). I had also been a head of department but the Vice-Chancellor had only ever offered me the lowest level of merit payment. The third letter 'rectified that anomaly'. When I stepped down as dean I went in person to see the finance chap in charge of salaries to make sure my successor (a professor) had got his honorarium. He looked it up and told me that not only had my successor got his whack, his honorarium was double what I had been getting (£12K rather than 6).

The law profession is another that might be expected to be alert to discrimination within its own practices, if only for its reputation. But here is testimony given to a UK parliamentary commission on Women and Work by Fiona Woolf, a woman in a good position to comment:

'I then became president of the Law Society and we looked at the equal pay of the legal profession as an issue and discovered that, after lots of corrections for different types of work and different regions of the country, we still had a 7.9% pay gap in the legal profession, which was outrageous when you thought about the profession it was.'[4]

Ms Woolf has reason to continue to be concerned: the latest study of young graduates tells us that, of all the subjects, law shows the highest gender pay gap, described as some 40 years behind in its crawl to pay equity — not exactly the model employment sector.[5]

Finance, of course, is notorious for its testosterone-charged dealings at the mega-earning level but, even in the calmer waters of small-time lending, UK banks discriminate against female entrepreneurs, cramping the chances of women putting their competences to work for themselves.[6]

In Australia's legal services industry, recent statistics from the Workplace Gender Equality Agency show a 35.6% gender pay gap across all occupations, and a 13.9% gender pay gap between male and female senior managers specifically. It is not a like-for-like analysis of women and men doing the same job, so we cannot draw any far-reaching conclusions in regard to discrimination, but the lack of parity these figures seem to suggest cannot be overlooked.[7] Just as Ms Woolf remarked from within the heart of the United Kingdom's legal profession, so the Hon. Michael Kirby spoke, in an address to the Women Lawyers' Association of New South Wales during his period as a Justice of the High Court, of the lack of female lawyers speaking on High Court matters.[8]

Undoubtedly, however, the form of discrimination at work that has the deepest effect on women's careers is the bias against part-time employees. Working part-time usually means an immediate pay penalty. Over the working life, this adds up to tens, even hundreds, of thousands of dollars or pounds. The albatross accompanies a woman into her retirement, as her pension will be far smaller as a result. (Women's pensions across Europe are 34% below men's; in the United States, women's public pensions are 40% lower.[9]) The pay gap between full- and part-timers is bigger in the United Kingdom than in most OECD countries. As well as the material penalty, there is the symbolic penalisation. If you work part-time, you are not regarded as a serious career candidate; your chances of a promotion shrivel.[10]

Bias against part-time workers is illegal in the Netherlands. This is an example of an exceptionally fast turnaround for women's work: three decades ago, the Dutch were low down in the international tables of female employment. The educational crossover took place in the Netherlands as elsewhere, and Dutch women became much more active economically, very often in a part-time capacity. So, to avoid losing talent, the government passed legislation enforcing strong rights for part-timers to enjoy equal career opportunities.[11] Now, nearly two in three Dutch women aged 20 to 65 are in work. Almost three-quarters of them work part-time — but the average part-time week is 26 hours; this, combined with legislative support, means that part-time careers are far more of an option than in the United Kingdom, where the hours are shorter and the legislative framework much weaker.

As direct discrimination declines, less direct forms of discrimination have sprung up. Some of these will strike future generations as just as bizarre as the marriage bar now appears to us, but we are for the most part not aware of them. This is because discrimination is often, perhaps now mostly, unconscious. We all tend to prefer things that are familiar to us, and this includes who we select to work with us. Daniel Kahneman's Nobel Prize–winning research on priming and framing (unrecognised influences that shape our preferences) shows how easily we reach conclusions, and act on them, through processes that bear little relation to rational thought.[12] We don't need a Freudian account of recruitment practices to tell us that sex and rationality don't always go together. So some men (and some women) will reject women for jobs or promotions, even though this goes against such objective selection criteria as may exist.

Take a group of empirically minded, highly trained, and constantly ratiocinating scientists. Locate these scientists in Sweden, the Valhalla of gender equality. Give them a set of medical research papers, accompanying postdoctoral students' applications for research fellowships. Surely these scientists will judge the applications objectively, and gender neutrally? Well, it seems not — or not unless you anonymise the applications, removing the authors' names. An experiment along these lines carried out in 1995 caused shock waves in the Swedish scientific community when it revealed that, compared with the average male applicant, a female scientist had to be 2.6 times more productive if both were to be perceived as equally competent.[13] This corresponded to publishing 20 extra scientific publications in excellent specialist journals — a colossal difference, as authoring that number of papers needs years of work. The study led to a significant revision in the way research papers, on which the careers of women scientists depend, are judged in Sweden.

A US study addressed the same issue, using a randomised trial to test judgements of the same CV submitted for a science research post under male and female names. It produced broadly similar results to the Swedish experiment. Even scientists — female as well as male — who presumably pride themselves on their objectivity favoured the 'male' applicant for the post by a significant margin (though they were more likely to say they liked the 'female'). Furthermore, they were less rather than more likely to want to mentor the 'female' applicant if 'she' was successful.[14] Who knows how often this pattern is reproduced, despite the best efforts of those involved?

- IS IT BECAUSE I AM A WOMAN THAT I AM PAID LESS THAN A MAN?

- NOT AT ALL, IT IS BECAUSE YOU'RE NOT A MAN!

Sex by subject

Across OECD countries, overall discrimination in education has shrunk. We saw this in Chapter 2. Attitudes to girls achieving and going on to higher education have turned around — if anything, it may be boys who suffer from low expectations — but there is still significant gender discrimination in education through subject choice. This remains a real barrier, with girls discouraged in various ways from studying traditionally male subjects.[15]

Advice and guidance on subject and career choice are a vital link between learning and work. This goes far beyond the formal sessions offered in a careers office, at school, or at college.[16] It's about how girls and boys have subject and career opportunities presented to them: the way these opportunities are talked about, modelled, and valued, especially in informal settings. Does Paula get offered the full spectrum, or is she pushed away from some of the opportunities? There's simply no doubt that pushing away still goes on; so does the more or less gentle pulling in to more 'gender-familiar' subjects and careers such as hairdressing or nursing.

We know girls are less likely to choose sciences, engineering, and maths, and more likely to choose arts and humanities subjects. How far is social conditioning responsible, or are these choices shaped more by factors whose roots go deep into our evolutionary past? This is a capital-B big issue but I shall skate quickly across it. There will always be some degree of difference in the overall choices made by girls and boys. To some, lesser, extent these will reflect deep-seated, inbuilt, and genuine predilections. But these overall patterns should not lead anyone into assuming that *individual* young women have a particular preference or talent of a kind that marks them out from boys (and vice-versa). The two sexes largely overlap in their tastes and dispositions, and the overlap will become bigger still as more is done to enable genuine choice. The overlap will never be total, but it will be significant. The problem is that young women are still covertly channelled and actively steered away from particular subjects in ways that constrict their career choices and their earning opportunities. Young men are subject to similar pressures — for instance, making it very difficult for them to work with young children — though in their case the financial penalties at least are less severe.

There are subjects where there is almost total segregation, and it matters materially that the subjects from which girls are most deterred are often those that bear the most financial reward. Hairdressing apprentices in the United Kingdom are paid about £110 per week on average (median), and 92% of them are women; in Australia, the figure is around $626 per week, and 86% are women. Engineering apprentices are paid £240 a week, and 97% of them are men; in Australia, electrician apprentices are paid around $691 an hour, and 98.6% of them are men.[17] These are the extremes, but women on average earn 21% less than men in the apprenticeship sector.[18] Science and engineering degrees earn significantly more for their graduates than arts ones do.

So should we only be content when half of the students in each subject area are male and half female? Or would it be reasonable to extend the boundaries to 60/40, or 70/30?[19] I've already said that I consider the 50/50 solution as not just impracticable but also actively running counter to a reasoned approach to gender balance (other than possibly to kickstart a process of greater equality). We know that men and women do not fall into two discrete groups, but overlap far more than they differ in their attitudes and capacities. We also know that gender is not the only significant divider, so if we have 50/50 on gender, the logic is for other characteristics, such as race, to be treated similarly. Result: contortions and distortions, especially where there are not just two categories but several, as with ethnicity. For me, a two-thirds/one-third split across different subjects is a sensible threshold (whether the two-thirds are women or men in each particular subject).[20] If this is breached, in either direction, then it needs looking into. If not, there are probably more important things to worry about.

Careers at the council

Lily, Maureen, and Edna work for a county council. They are all in what they call late middle age, and have worked for the council for about 60 years between them: Lily as manager of a residential care home for children, Maureen in property records, and Edna in the careers service, Youth Connexions. When I met them, we were joined in our discussion by Felicity, a generation younger, who works for the public service union at the council.

The older women do not have degrees, unlike Felicity. They are highly pragmatic about their working careers. They do not think they could ever have risen to professional heights, but they are firmly aware of their competences — and of the incompetence of others senior to them. Maureen joined the council from working in a bank, because as a single mother, she needed to earn more money. 'Stupidly, I thought coming to county I'd start on a higher salary and so there would be more career opportunity. I like what I do, though I am aware that when they took me on they thought of me as a middle-aged woman who would just sit there quietly and get on with the filing,' she says.

'It was clear that's what they thought of me — "Give her a pat on the head and she'll be all right." For the first three years, my manager wasn't really interested in what I did or said … Another manager was four grades above me, and he had the title of database manager, but I had to show him how to use a database. I have recently got my manager to agree to look at a pay review. After three years, it's a bit late, but finally it's being looked at.'

Lily arrived at our meeting hotfoot from a minor emergency in the care home that she manages. The home caters for troubled young people, and some of them had broken some equipment. Lily is highly critical of the way the system operates: after such incidents, the damaged kit is simply replaced, and the children never learn what life outside involves in the way of costs, so they are unprepared for the rigours of independent living. She is confident of her own competences, even though she has little in the way of formal qualifications. 'I had the minimum qualification needed for my job, an NVQ level 3, but I hit every bullet point. I supervise three people and I'm responsible for the catering, for the fabric of the home, and for what goes in the kids' rooms. You don't need a degree to do what I do. You need to be a plate-spinner — and I'm a very good plate-spinner.'

She considers herself well paid. She has been thinking of looking at other jobs because she can't rise any higher in her current one, but if she changed jobs she would either have a significant drop in salary or be obliged to move to a different area: 'To go further, I'd have to go out of county or look for two grades above. To go further, I'd have to leave a job that I'm very, very good at and that I like, and I have to ask, would I be doing that because there's another job I like, or because I want the money? Sometimes it's not about the money.'

Like Maureen, Lily has reservations about the competence of those above her — but for rather different reasons. All her bosses are women, who have worked their way up through the grades. She says there is a serious groupthink problem when all managers are women, and part of a tight-knit group: 'I call them "the coven". They came through the ranks together. There's a kind of shield around them. I made my own manager promise me not to join the coven.'

Edna's managers seem more supportive, in a changing work context: 'We have had to become target-driven. But I still love my job, and I'm still being pushed to develop by my managers. I'm at the top of where I can get to, but I don't necessarily want to change. My manager's just twisted my arm to do another qualification, I think maybe to keep me happy. I don't know if it's going to help me, but it looks good on her record — and the fact that it's me that they've chosen to push forward is nice.'

Felicity, the degree-holder, has been the most disappointed of them all: 'In 13 years I've been for so many jobs, but always seemed to come second. I was offered a couple, but I didn't like what I heard about them, and I didn't want to grab just anything.' She did a secondment, at three grades higher, and got glowing reports, but this didn't seem to count for anything afterwards. 'I was working in IT, I was made a lot of promises … I did a whole load of studying, anything to enhance my prospects, but somehow it hasn't worked out. Ironically, I'm now working full-time for the union. I'm happy as Larry, even though it's poorly paid.'

County councils are bureaucracies. They have to be — they are large public organisations, and need to be structured in a recognisable and accountable way. Let's not forget that when Max Weber first introduced the notion of bureaucracies, they were organisations that were designed to undermine the old systems of patronage, and open up careers to all talents. In that sense, a bureaucracy should prevent discrimination: it should operate according to clear and transparent procedures in to which people are promoted for what they can do, not whom they know.

The women saw it a little differently. As Edna put it: 'When you work for [the council], they don't promote you for what you can do. You have to go through a very rigorous process. It's not very pleasant. I suppose because we're a county council there are certain procedures, it's not just what you can do. But it's still old school, about who you know, whether your face fits.'

The three older women are from the generation that mainly missed out on the expansion of post-school education, and on the success of their daughters' generation. They do not seem to resent that they did not have the same educational opportunities. But they do resent the way that formal qualifications are required for jobs that they believe they can do perfectly well anyway. Maureen said: 'There's an age thing, as well as a woman thing. Many of these qualifications didn't exist when I was at school. Asking for a degree is a very clever way of filtering out women of our age. When we were young, most women didn't go to university. So this increasing need to have a degree discriminates against people — most of them women — who are older and never went for a degree. The chances are they couldn't go or didn't want to go.'

Lily added: 'Nowadays you can get a degree in project management. Well, I'm sorry, but in my book that's called "being capable".'

And Edna chimed in: 'A lot of it is down to common sense, which I'm afraid is often missing with what goes on here, or down at [the council's headquarters].'

There is a certain irony here — in fact, a multiple irony. The introduction of formally recognised qualifications should drive down discrimination, but for this group it has had the reverse impact. There is a generation effect: older women who worked their way up, garnering experience but without having it endorsed and physically embodied in those framed certificates, have found themselves bypassed by those who have the requisite paperwork. This has now changed, as women get more qualifications, and in future it is more likely to be older men than older women who will not have the qualifications. Those who go through life with no qualifications will have a difficult ride.

But the increasing demand from bosses for qualifications may devalue the kinds of competence — common sense, capability — that women particularly pride themselves on. Lily's rejection of 'project management' as something you can be trained in (or maybe she just meant you don't need to do a full degree in it) epitomises this. On the one hand, one reason that women are more likely to take part in formal training is that they know that they need to demonstrate that they have learnt a particular competence; they are much less likely than men to rely on just asserting that they can do whatever it is that needs to be done. On the other hand, they can often draw on a more diverse set of experiences that are simply not able to be formally recognised, such as the organisational skills and capacity for multi-tasking that managing a household with children often demands. So the whole process of certification is something of a double-edged sword for Paula.

Moreover, the procedures that are designed to identify and reward competence don't seem to have fully displaced the reliance on personal contacts or sponsors. Edna said: 'I worked in personnel for six years in the days when everything was manual, and I'd be photocopying 15 copies of all the applications. I'd ask my boss why we were doing this when everyone knew Joe Soap would get the job — and he said, "You and I both know, but we have to be seen to be doing it this way." It's very wrong. And I think it often doesn't help women.'

She is talking about goings-on from a long time ago, but the sentiment Edna expressed featured strongly in the discussions I had with women currently working in other bureaucracies, such as those from the central civil service (see Chapter 7).

In a different working environment, the BBC, Florence was just moving from her job as a radio producer. She said: 'We have a very antiquated system of review boards. It's just internal interviews, which stylistically tends to favour men. It doesn't put any checks and balances in place to counter the de facto exercise of power. There is a whole series of tick boxes in the procedure, but if you look at what actually happens, the editors are generally men, and the foot soldiers are women. The "ideas-y" jobs, being a sounding-board for ideas — these tend to be for men, and the women tend to get the handholding jobs, like soothing difficult presenters, so you've got the safe-maternal-hands work versus the blue-skies-thinking kind of work.'

Olivia echoed this, but from a different angle. She is in her early 30s, and now works as a strategist in a major branding consultancy, after several years making documentaries. Like Florence, Olivia found in her filmmaking career that young men are given the juicier roles, though she notes that this is changing: 'There's a perception in film that men are more suited to more technical roles — they'll be better able to edit or shoot film — and they'll be given those opportunities. It's older men running the editing suites or the labs, and they don't expect you to know about these. I don't think I was that affected. I just thought it's a generation thing.'

In her current workplace, the agency has prided itself on a distinctive and non-bureaucratic organisational culture: 'There's no transparency about what people get paid, so there are rumours, and that's not helpful. There's supposedly no hierarchy, but in fact there is one. The slogan is "high empathy, low organisation", but they are growing as an organisation and it can't go on like that.'

They've recently introduced an HR director, who has brought in a more systematic approach to rewards. Olivia now has someone she feels she can go to and raise this kind of issue. It's a small example of the positive side of bureaucratisation.

The importance of being valued

One further theme emerged very strongly from the discussion with Lily, Maureen, and Edna. All were single parents and all have made a career for themselves, but it has been a struggle to get their work recognised, and to find a career path. This is why their promotions mean a lot to them, materially but also personally. Discrimination has quite an intimate and subtle relationship to how people are valued more generally — and especially to how they value themselves. Here the county-council women had very particular stories to tell from their domestic circumstances, and the memories they have of their ex-husbands' attitudes towards their potential. All their husbands had recognised their intelligence, but could not make the further step to seeing them as having serious jobs with prospects. Edna said: 'My ex-husband always said I could have been a barrister. But he never thought about doing anything to help my career.'

All had been involved in some kind of voluntary work, usually connected with their children's schools. They had valued this, and felt appreciated by those on the receiving end — but not by their husbands: 'Being a school governor filled a massive hole. I felt valued; people said, "Thank you." Whereas my ex-husband never valued me as someone doing something for other people,' said Maureen. That attitude may be changing with the generations, but there is still a major issue around how we value work other than through the amount that is paid for doing it.

In short, we could think of three overlapping spheres where women's competences are (or are not) recognised: the workplace, the home, and the community. The Paula Principle relates primarily to the first of these: how far women's competences are recognised at work. But this cannot be completely disentangled from how their competences are valued elsewhere. To know that their skills and work are valued in the community helps protect women against negative judgements elsewhere, and can sustain their belief in their capacities.[21]

The county-council women's experience differs from the journalist Nuala's in at least two respects. As a political journalist, she operates at a higher professional level than they do; and the practical issue of promotions means more to them than to Nuala, with her freelance background. But there is a very strong common theme: that the 'value' of their work is something they judge independently of formal or bureaucratic arrangements. This is not simply a matter of who does or does not feel underpaid. It is that they operate almost within two discrete scales, or frameworks: the system that pays them, and their own intrinsic sense of what competences they are putting into practice. When these two are out of sync, and *if* they become aware of this disjuncture, then it is painful. And it is more likely to happen for women than men.

Diminishing discrimination: a matter of time?

Discrimination in the workplace is contentious and difficult ground. The high-profile cases tend to be about professional high-flyers. It is harder to find evidence from less rarified occupational levels, and yet discrimination may be more severe there, even if it grabs less attention. It does not seem to be diminishing: Acas, the advisory, conciliation, and arbitration service, received 7,175 sex discrimination-related calls to its helpline in the year to the end of March 2016 — a 14% increase on the previous year.[22] In a recent UK survey, around one in nine expectant mothers reported that they felt forced to leave their job. This included those being dismissed; made compulsorily redundant, where others in their workplace were not; or — the most common reason — feeling they were being treated so poorly that they had to leave their job. If scaled up to the population as a whole, this would mean something over 50,000 women lost their jobs because of pregnancy, and that's a large number by any standard.[23] In Australia, a staggering one in two pregnant women and mothers returning to work said they had experienced discrimination. Discrimination in this survey, which was conducted by the Human Rights Commission, included fewer career opportunities, as well as compulsory redundancies, reduced pay or responsibility, and negative attitudes from others. One in three of those women who said they had experienced discrimination had either resigned or started looking for another job as a result.[24]

A visible source of discrimination

In Chapter 3, we saw how enduring the gender gap is in pay and in careers. This is prima facie evidence for discrimination, especially as women's levels of qualification rise. In addition to the material fact of the current gender pay gap, women wait longer for promotions than do equivalent men, even when factors such as job experience are controlled for. Once they get to supervisory or managerial level, they wait longer for further promotions. Switching jobs in mid-career is more difficult, as age counts against women more.[25] And so on.

As for skill use, the overall message from an OECD study is quite explicit: 'There are generally more women than men in jobs that do not make full use of their literacy and numeracy skills … Women are traditionally disadvantaged, not least in labour markets, which may point to more systematic underutilisation of their skills based on discrimination and other allocation mechanisms that are operating on the labour market.'[26]

What are the mechanisms through which this works? University of Manchester academics Damian Grimshaw and Jill Rubery provide a particularly useful '5-V' framework for which women's skills are undergraded.

- Visibility: women's skills are not recognised, either directly, because they are not accredited, or indirectly, because women are concentrated in occupations that don't command attention.
- Valuation: jobs done by women are less valued.
- Vocation: women are regarded as 'called to' their work, and so less in need of recognition and reward.
- Value-added: women's jobs are less likely to be in the technically high-value-added areas — personal care is a telling example.
- Variance: women's work is more likely to deviate from the full-time continuous model.[27]

You could use this framework to form your own assessment of the extent of discrimination against women, and how likely change will be.

Self-discrimination

Who does the discriminating? We naturally assume that, in the case of gender, the discriminators are men. This must be the case generally: men are still likely to be either the sole authority or in the majority in decisions on appointments, promotions, pay awards, and so on. Women also discriminate, particularly perhaps women who have reached male-dominated positions and consciously or not share male assumptions. But less obvious and more intriguing is the idea that women discriminate against themselves — self-discrimination being on a parallel with self-censorship.

'Is it possible to discriminate unfairly against oneself?' sounds like an undergraduate philosophy question, but it focuses the attention on who has what actual and potential choices, and whether these are distributed in a way that we regard as fair and reasonable. It involves thinking about the factors that shape our preferences as well as about actual abilities.[28] The notion of self-discrimination, therefore, overlaps substantially with PP factor three, confidence (or lack thereof), as well as PP factor five, choice. If women refuse to put themselves forward for jobs or promotions, are they making a genuine, if possibly regrettable, judgement, or could they be more accurately described as acting against their own self-interest, and, even more cruelly, against the interests of women generally? That would be a harsh judgement indeed, but there is something there to debate. 'Self-handcuffing' was how Wilma, an interviewee we will meet later, referred to this process, using the term as much against herself as her fellows. Who has the key to this particular set of handcuffs? It's a real, not a rhetorical, question.

Even though the explanation for the Paula Principle cannot simply be discrimination, discrimination of some kind will very often be part of it. This is why the diagram on page 77 in this chapter is useful; it draws attention to how the different factors interact with one another. Arguably, for example, inadequate childcare or eldercare provision in workplace contracts is discriminatory, as are practices that undermine women's self-confidence, and networks that exclude them. The next chapter tries to unpick some of these prickly connections.

5

Explaining the Paula Principle

Factor two — caring responsibilities

There are external constraints that inhibit or prevent women from taking on career challenges, or even from contemplating them in the first place. By far the most insistent of these is children. Girls and boys might resent being labelled as constraints, but having children does tend to put a lifetime brake on a mother's earnings and to set her on a lower career trajectory, however good the employer is on child-friendly arrangements and however cooperative the father is in sharing childcare (and, of course, excluding how delightful the compensations of motherhood may be).

Later in life, and increasingly as we survive longer, ageing parents and family members impinge on what might have been the later, higher-earning years of a woman's career. Eldercare looms over the horizon just as childcare fades, or even overlaps with it. How caring responsibilities are divided among family members, and between them and external providers of care such as crèches or care homes, is a fundamental conditioner of women's careers. PP factor two, caring responsibilities, accounted for 27% of website votes, so let's examine it in more detail.

Children: the asteroid effect

It is not surprising that caring responsibilities received more votes on the website than any other as an explanatory factor for the Paula Principle. It is women's childbearing capacity that lies behind all the social arrangements and attitudes underlying the Paula Principle. It affects childless women of childbearing age as well as mothers, because of actual or potential employers' expectations that they might want children at some point.

Brenda has strong views on the matter. 'I would say that this is getting worse rather than better — because of the cost. I say to young women who are trying to think through all this, and are faced with the prospect that childcare costs are going to take up practically their entire net salary, "You just have to look on this as a long-term investment; look at your career over a lifetime, and it's hugely, hugely harder if you leave."'

Brenda moved on from a very successful civil-service career to become a mentor and coach for women in mid-career. She has two children herself, now adults, and is forthright on the lack of affordable good-quality childcare in the United Kingdom. The march towards better childcare, she says, has been thrown into reverse gear. This means that often women are now working almost for nothing, in a narrow economic sense: they bring in little to no net income, once the childcare costs are factored in. Brenda's advice to mothers is to focus on the returns that will come in the future: the careers they have so strenuously maintained will take them on up the ladder, and the childcare costs will shrink once the children go off to school. She also underlines that financial reward is only one reason women work; they also want to put their abilities to use, and to have an identity beyond that of a full-time mother.

Brenda's clients are professionally qualified women, with senior careers in prospect. Their patience and sacrifice have a fair chance of being rewarded later on. In addition, if they are in a partnership, it is very likely to be with a professional man who earns a decent salary; this 'assortative mating' of educational equals is a major driver of inequality between households, as Alison Wolf argues.[1] For many other women who do not operate at this level, both their current situation and their future prospects look very different. They may have qualifications, but not ones that lead to a career in the high-earning professional classes. So not only do they earn less now, with childcare costs swallowing up a larger proportion of their current earnings, but their 'investment' does not even materialise later; although they continue to work, they are not on an upward path that will eventually increase their earnings.

– MY STOCK DEALING IS GOING FINE. MY WIFE TELLS ME SHE'S INVESTED IN CHILD CARE, BUT I'M NOT SURE HOW THAT'S WORKING OUT.

Objectively, motherhood seems the easiest factor to quantify as an explanation for the Paula Principle. The impact is measurable, both over time and between generations. We can see this from comparing two major studies that have tracked thousands of women from birth — one cohort born in 1958, one in 1970.[2] The news is certainly not all bad: over time, women have become less likely to slide down a job level or two after having a child than used to be the case. Nearly one in three first-time mothers born in 1958 experienced downward occupational mobility on their first return to work, but for mothers born in 1970, the figure dropped to one in seven. This is real progress in reducing the career penalty paid by women for having children.[3]

But now for the sting: the penalties on women who take a *part-time* job after their first childbirth have *increased* in the same period. Nearly one in five women who return to full-time work after the birth of their first child drop down the occupational ladder, but the figure is nearly one in two for those who return part-time.[4] We're not talking only about professional high-flyers, though this is where it may show up most acutely. The effect occurs at all occupational levels.

Here, women in the United Kingdom are disproportionately affected, so it is not surprising that childcare came out as the top factor underlying the Paula Principle among UK website voters. Childcare in the United Kingdom is among the most expensive in the Western world. Parents in the UK spend 33% of their net household income on childcare, compared with an OECD average of 13%.[5] In the Netherlands, where, as in the United Kingdom, there are high levels of women in part-time employment, childcare costs are typically under 10% of the household income. In Australia in 2015, the average out-of-pocket expense on childcare was between 9 and 11% of income (with lower-income families paying more proportionally).[6] The United Kingdom sits uncomfortably between two groups of European countries: ones, mainly in Northern Europe, which have high levels of state provision of childcare; and ones, mainly around the Mediterranean, where mothers can still rely on family support for looking after children (this latter, of course, generally means other women). British women often can't rely on mother or mother-in-law to look after the baby, but can't afford the alternative either. In job terms, they pay heavily for this.

In 2014, the cost of sending a child under two to nursery part-time (25 hours) was well over £100 per week in Britain. For a family with two children in full-time childcare, the typical yearly bill is over £11,000. This makes childcare costs 62% higher than the cost of the average mortgage for a family home. Over the last five years, childcare costs have risen 27%.[7] In many cases, the cost completely deters women from taking paid employment, as the amount left over after paying childcare is derisory, once the effects of losing benefits is factored in.[8]

The direct cost is accentuated by the sheer incoherence of the benefits system. Take a household where the primary wage earner — let's assume it is a man — is a low-income earner and his partner wants to take up employment. The loss of benefit is so penal that, if she is also a low-earner, they will be no better off until she works more than 30 hours a week. And just how much better off will they then be? Working full-time, she will make a £700 net gain in household income *for the entire year*. You could think of it as a dizzyingly high marginal tax rate that often rises to 80% of income and not infrequently tops 100%. This is a levy that puts tax-tormented millionaires in the comfortable shade. While this kind of absurdity particularly affects women in poorly paid occupations, the disincentives are still strong for many who are better off. Even those qualified at higher levels struggle — especially single parents, as Becky's case illustrates (see her story on page 108).

Increasingly, it looks as if women may choose not to have children if there is no adequate and affordable childcare. This explains the at-first surprising demographic trend of birth rates being much lower for women in Catholic countries in southern Europe than for those in secular or Protestant countries in northern Europe, where contraception has long been sanctioned. Italian Paulas, for example, are keen on careers (maybe partly because they are in families that feel obliged to support 30-year-old, stay-at-home young Pietros, but that's another story), and many will not embark on motherhood if it puts paid to their chances of work. Women have a more positive experience in Scandinavia, where quasi-universal childcare is relatively cheap and so enables women to have both children and careers.

The competence cross-over, with women now representing so much more of the nation's human capital, casts the issue of childcare in a new light, bright enough to illuminate starkly that inadequate provision means a massive waste of talent. This collective loss of talent mirrors the individual penalty paid. The mutually reinforcing combination of part-time employment, low income, a horrendously complex and often perverse benefits system, and unaffordable or unavailable childcare is toxic. The price that women pay for having children continues over decades. It resembles a debt with an arbitrary interest rate where the principal cannot be paid off.

This is precisely why, when it comes to a Paula Agenda — what needs to be done to undermine the Paula Principle — the focus has to be on work and careers *in a life-course perspective* (see Chapter 9). Better childcare; more parental leave, shared to a greater extent by fathers; and a fairer division of domestic responsibilities will all help to soften the asteroid impact that the arrival of children often has on mothers' careers. But the crucial thing in the longer term is that women must be able to get back onto whatever path best suits their competences, even if that happens years after they have given birth. This requires a different approach to working time generally, not just when children are there to be cared for. I come back to this later in the book.

The catch-22: Becky's story

Becky works 28 hours as an office manager, four days a week. Her childcare costs for her three-year-old are £565 a month, and she receives the maximum 80% support, up to the £175 per week limit. Changes in the United Kingdom welfare regulations mean that Becky is losing over £1,300 a year in support.

'This will be very, very hard for me,' she laments. 'I was going to try and set up a pension, but I won't be able to afford those payments every month now. I've already cut down on all our non-essential spending, so the only way to get around these costs is to try and negotiate working a shorter day, from 9.30 to 2.30, so I don't have to use childcare at all — although this will mean I work fewer hours and so I earn less.

'I honestly have no idea how I'm going to manage with this. I am a manager, I'm well qualified, I have 11 years' experience — I contribute to my local economy through my skills and experience. But I feel that I'm being forced to consider giving this up. What example does this teach my daughter — that it's better to give in and have no aspirations rather than to struggle as a working mother?'

Time-juggling, role-modelling, and intergenerational effects are all here. Even Becky's future pension is shrinking as a result; the career effects that I'm talking about extend well beyond the end of working lives, so any measurement of the cumulative impact of lower career trajectories should include the literally lifelong effect.[9]

The very fact, or simply the possibility, of having children conditions attitudes towards women in the workplace. Donna works as a careers advisor. As she said to me, fingering the silver engagement ring on her finger: 'In an interview, when you are 25 like me, you know your employer will be looking at your ring and he'll be thinking, "Is she going to have a baby any time soon?" even though he's not allowed to ask it.' Although she has always been lucky with her employers, she is aware that many women aren't so lucky.

Brenda was stunned by a telling incident early on in her career. After the birth of her first child, she returned quickly to work. Before her pregnancy, she normally cycled there along a busy road in South London that culminated in a major roundabout, but now that she was a mother, she decided the safety risks entailed in this were too big to take. When she told this to a senior colleague, whom she regarded as extremely intelligent, he responded to her in mock-amazement, 'I didn't know Peter [her son] had a mother.'

I had taped my interview with Brenda and, when I listened back to the recording, this struck me as such an extraordinarily strange thing to say that I specifically checked it back with her. She confirmed it; the episode had made such a tremendous impact on her that even after 30 years she remembered it word for word. The clue may be in the contrast with the colleague's own domestic setup; his wife stayed at home as a full-time mother to their children, and my assumption is that his remark was an instinctive, subconscious defence of that, if a wantonly barbed and hurtful one. Until then Brenda, from a single-sex school and with a good university experience behind her, had had little time for most complaints about discrimination. This changed her outlook. How far her colleague's outlook has changed — and those of his successors — is another matter.

Juggling on the high wire

Sharing the caring time

Let's switch the focus away from financial cost. There is no reason why childcare should be solely the mother's responsibility, or one shared between only her and those providing the care from outside the family, whether publicly or privately. There is another figure lurking somewhere in the picture. Fathers do now take more responsibility than they used to, often with enthusiasm. Paternity leave is available in the United Kingdom and in many other countries, and fathers play a much bigger part generally in the raising of children. But this 'more' and 'bigger' are relative to the past, where their role in day-to-day childcare has historically been minimal.

Househusbands exist. They always have: Donna told me how her father gave up his job as an established engineer three decades ago to look after his four daughters while his wife went out to work as a teacher. 'He wasn't a particularly feminine man, you know, he was a rugby player. But there were lots of things about that which were good for us — we had a rational father figure at home, so we'd come home and cry on his shoulder and he'd say, "Well, let's have a look at what we can do about this."'

Full-time househusbands are always likely to be a small minority. Here are the stories of two couples, which show two different attitudes — and outcomes.

Dora and Dieter are German. They live in London and have three small children: Oliver, six; Nick, three; and Margaret, 18 months. Dieter is head of marketing for a financial institution. Dora went to a *realschule*, a type of German secondary school that focuses on practical skills, but unusually she transferred from this to a more academic school (clearly because she was intellectually capable, though she was too modest to say this). After school, she started business studies but then switched to computer sciences at a technical university deep in the Black Forest, where she was the only girl in the class.[10] She met Dieter, came to London with him when he relocated for his job, and worked in telecoms. After a while, she returned to Germany to finish her studies and then came back to London to complete her diploma in information technology. Since starting a job in telecoms in 2006, she has had two promotions and is now a project manager for a large company.

Dora resumed her career recently, when her youngest child was just 18 months. 'Up until having children, I was quite ambitious, but when I had two children I took quite an undemanding job so I could leave at five o'clock — not very stimulating. Moving to my current job means that I can now think about my career again.' Ambition, for her, is not only or even primarily about aiming to get higher; it's about having a job that is reasonably stretching.

Dora works 27 hours a week. She is contactable to colleagues outside her hours, and doesn't seem to resent this — in fact, she is proud of it, seeing it as a positive sign of her work commitment. Computing technology is a good business for women because it offers opportunities for greater flexibility, such as being able to work from home and operate a variable schedule. Despite this flexibility, she reports, as many women do, that since having children she has had to be more focused, knowing that 5.00 pm is a firmly fixed cut-off point that she can't go beyond. She calls it 'a hard stop'. Going for a drink after work has to be arranged a week ahead, which means that she misses some of the office networking, but she doesn't resent this.

The 'hard stop' mentality is about daily and weekly schedules: how parents organise their time. The idea that women have more of a capacity to multitask is pretty well established — we all know the image of a woman taking a work call while getting packed lunches ready for the children and at the same time thinking how to arrange for mother-in-law to come and stay for a couple of days next week, or a similar variant.[11] But it may be helpful to think of this capacity as demonstrating greater flexibility in putting together disparate elements of a career that does not fit the 'standard' continuous and full-time pattern, and coping with the effects when life does not conform to expectations.

Dieter had been going through an unhappy time at work, so Dora suggested he might go part-time for a while. She thought that it might also help him understand a bit more about her own balancing act: he would see more clearly the effort required to juggle work and kids and — just as importantly — how determined she was to continue upwards in her career and combine this with a large family. On top of that, she hoped it would enable him to become a little less defined by his work, and achieve a better work–life balance. Dieter's response was one of incomprehension rather than rejection: it seems that her suggestion never really made actual sense to him. Shifting to part-time, even as a temporary move, was simply not an idea that gained any purchase on his imagination. It's important to say that Dora did not make these remarks in any tone of complaint about her husband. Her comment seems to reflect just how hard men find it to understand the nature of women's work commitments. What did upset her were those managers at work who either thought that because she had a young child she would not be interested in a particular position, or that if a woman moves to four days a week she would not be in the frame for managerial jobs.

Freda and Tim have very different attitudes to careers and parenting from Dora and Dieter. I talked with them both in a Patisserie Valerie café in central London, while their three-year-old son, Victor, was intermittently occupied with foamy babyccinos and cake. Freda has been with an arts company promoting circus activity for ten years. She has worked her way steadily upwards, with a promotion roughly every two years, and now has a team of six working for her. She wants to move beyond circus into a field with broader artistic reach and greater impact.

Tim has worked in a London theatre for ten years, for the last seven of them as a technical manager. He grew up in Chichester, with its well-known theatre, which inspired him to want to go into the industry, and so studied at the London Academy of Music and Drama. There he got experience in a variety of roles: sound, lighting, wardrobe. Stage management might have been the obvious choice for a career, but he knew that was not for him. He has never been conventionally ambitious — to the point where this became a source of some friction in earlier days, as Freda, with her outlook, thought he should be aiming higher. She nudged him into going to university to get a degree, though Tim says he was happy in what he was doing and did not feel stuck.

'We used to have a lot of arguments about ambition,' says Freda. 'I just found it unbelievable that Tim could be happy with his lot, which was me and a middle-level job in the theatre. That wouldn't be enough for me, and still isn't enough for me, so at the time I found it really frustrating. It was, like, what are our goals?' she says, looking earnest.

'And I,' Tim interjects, 'was going, "what's wrong with this?" It's not like I'm saying this is the last job I'll ever do.'

'It's not just that,' Freda quickly comes back at him. 'You don't want the extra responsibility. I've been saying you could take more of a leadership role, you could put yourself out there, and it's just not something that drives you.'

The difference in outlook between them has, however, turned out to be all for the best since they've had Victor. Tim positively wanted to be a hands-on dad, and was more than willing to arrange his work to do so. This was very much part of their negotiations and agreement when the possibility of having a child came up. Freda would not have accepted being mainly, let alone solely, responsible for the childcare. As a result, Tim went part-time when Victor was three months, enabling Freda to return to work full-time. Tim has since gone back to working full-time, but has very flexible hours and so can arrange things to fit with Freda's (and Victor's) timetable.

Freda sums it up: 'I used to find it really frustrating that Tim didn't have this sense of driving things forward, but in recent years it's obviously totally paid off because it means that I can exactly do what I choose while he can happily hold the fort and look after the baby. So it's worked out absolutely brilliantly.'

Eldercare

Earlier in this chapter, women's mentor and coach Brenda advised women to suck up the childcare costs: 'You just have to look on this as a long-term investment; look at your career over a lifetime, and it's hugely, hugely harder if you leave.' But things aren't even that straightforward anymore because, whereas caring used to be more or less wholly focused on children, now it looks both ways. Eldercare is a relatively new component of the care issue — or, rather, its scale and political profile are new. So many of us are living longer that the whole shape of our population is changing, with a different balance between generations. Inevitably, this means that many more older people already live with some kind of disability, or at least are in some measure unable to look after themselves fully. How do we, collectively, cope? It is more commonly women who take up the caring responsibilities for their own parents (or other elders) and, often, for those of their partner too. It is a significant issue: according to a report from the Institute of Public Policy Research, 'there are currently at least 315,000 working-age adults who have left work because of their caring responsibilities, and who remain outside of the labour market. Just under two-thirds (62%) of this group are women. This is estimated to cost Britain at least £1.3 billion a year in extra benefit spending and lost tax revenue.'[12]

In the United Kingdom, about two-thirds of a million women and a third of a million men receive the Carer's Allowance, which supports carers of disabled people (not only the elderly).[13] This is the formal end of the caring spectrum. It tells us little about those daily acts of support, which, even in the minds of those involved, might not figure as 'caring' in the technical sense, only in the emotional or practical sense — the popping in, the occasional shopping, the safety-netting where there is a crisis. This is the kind of activity that women do much more than men; they are the multitasking maintenance engineers of families and family relations. Across the

OECD, 10% of people aged over 50 provide some kind of care to the elderly. Two-thirds of these are women.[14] In Australia, 12% of the population is involved in caring for adults — 23% of all women. Most carers are in the 45–64 age group, and Australia is not alone in this.[15]

Eldercare raises again the question of 'voluntariness': how far caring for someone is a positive choice, or a matter of moral obligation or even compassion. These kinds of responsibilities especially affect later careers, as middle-aged women deal with elderly parents or other family members. Eldercare responsibilities may come just at the point when their career trajectory is turning upwards, after trundling along on the flat as their children grew up. The demands of eldercare are unpredictable — you cannot tell when, for how long, and with what degree of intensity care will be needed.

Vanessa, one of our North Easterners, now works 30 hours a week as a tax adviser for Her Majesty's Revenue and Customs (HMRC). Vanessa started with no qualifications. She has worked her way up, studying for a range of qualifications along the way, and is an enthusiastic proselytiser for adult learning. Where will it lead? 'I'd like to move on to something different — I'm not so sure about upwards.' She still firmly thinks of herself as having a career, despite the constraints of caring. It just doesn't have to involve vertical progression. She reduced her hours from full-time because she is caring for her mother. Her husband also suffers from ill health. Prioritising care-giving along with paid work, she feels, is a choice she has made. Her hours suit her, and allow her to manage the caring side. But she would like to change jobs, partly to get away from the stress (the job involves giving advice over the phone to anxious people struggling with their tax forms, helping them to add things up and fill in the forms correctly), but also because she wants to move on.

The debate on gendered eldercare lags far behind that on gendered childcare. The issues are not discussed as widely, and there is much less research on the full extent and nature of eldercare demands. In a way, this is entirely understandable, since the demographic trends that make it increasingly salient today are quite recent. But there is a very different complexion to the whole issue, since the biology of motherhood is not mirrored in eldercare; unlike giving birth, there is no evident a priori reason why eldercare should be unequally distributed between women and men. No breastfeeding is required; early bonding is achieved long ago. It is true that arguments about income foregone may still weigh in favour of men working rather than caring. They are still more likely to have the higher income, and therefore the household loses more if they give up or reduce their paid work. But the overall case for asymmetry in care responsibilities is far weaker. I sense that there is a much bigger debate looming around this issue — perhaps even opening up whole new areas of psychology to do with parent–child relations in later life, mirroring some of the last century's exploration of what happens in early childhood. Even simply recognising the fact of one's parents' physical or psychological dependency can be a telling moment. But that's an exploration for someone else to take forward.

In Claire Messud's 2014 novel, *The Woman Upstairs*, narrator Nora Eldridge's mother, intelligent and educated, has played the traditional domestic role of post-war society, raising two children and depending entirely on her husband financially. When Nora is seven, her mother is humiliated to discover that she does not have enough in her allowance to cover Christmas gifts: 'Suddenly — inexplicably to me as I was, but in a way so obvious to me now — she turned viperish, rageful: "Don't ever get yourself stuck like this," she hissed. "Promise me? Promise me now? … You need to have your own life, earn your own money, so you're not scrounging around like a beggar, trying to put ten dollars together for your kids' Christmas presents.

Leeching off your father's — your husband's — pathetic paycheck. Never. Never. Promise me?'

Nora fulfils the promise to her mother. She starts in management consultancy, where she has an office on the 34th floor and owns four pairs of Christian Louboutin shoes. She nearly marries her lawyer boyfriend, Ben. But by the time the novel opens, she has abandoned him and traded her status for a job as a teacher, all the time harbouring a secret desire to be an artist.

Some 25 years after the initial episode, Nora visits her mother, who is dying. At the end of the visit, her mother clenches her jaw and says: 'Get out. I can't. Get out. But never for a second think I don't remember what it's like. Don't think either that I can't help hating you for it. Just right now.'

In a sense, Nora has by then already got out. She has achieved the independence her mother craved. But the sadness of the story twines together the themes of family and career aspirations. Once Nora's mother dies, Nora takes on the main responsibility for looking after her ageing father, since her brother Matt is married and has his own family life.

Even as I was taking care of my parents, I got very good at practical things over those few years, like the most competent secretaries. I lived multiple lives: in the first, I had every appearance of a modestly accomplished young woman in her early 30s, capable if not interesting, easy to get on with, prompt, efficient, with unnoticeable clothes and a serviceable hairstyle …

My first life was a masquerade, my Clark Kent life, though in my second I was not a heroine at all. I sometimes hoped that someone out there imagined for me a second life of glamour and drama, as a rock star's mistress, or an FBI agent. But I wasn't the sort of person for whom anyone would bother imagining a secret life; and in that second life I was no lover or huntress or martyr, but a daughter, just a dutiful daughter.

Then there was my third life, small and secret: the life of my dioramas, the vestiges of my artist self.[16]

Nora's artistic specialty is making tiny elaborate dioramas, reconstructions of scenes from books, but she cannot make an independent living from it.

She sums it up:

You could say that my mother and father, grateful as they manifestly were, didn't ask me to give up my life. And if I chose to, though I can't see the logic of my own choice, I'd like to believe it was a purposeful choice and not simply a show of poor time management ... But you can't succeed in life unless you get good at it: there's no point in writing the world's best answer to the first question on the test, if you don't then leave yourself enough time to write any answers at all to the other questions. You still fail the test. And I worry, in my bleaker hours, that this is what I've done. I answered the dutiful daughter question really well; I was aware of doing only a so-so job on the grown-up career front, but I didn't really care, because there were two big exam questions I wanted to be sure I answered fully: the question of art, and the question of love.

The Woman Upstairs is a plangent story of a failure to resolve the timing question, and of how caring responsibilities — even if not exceptionally heavy in themselves — invade and undermine a woman's life. I say 'failure' because that's how Nora sees it. The story illustrates the Paula Principle, but not in a simple way. Nora had the chance of a high-earning career, and made the authentic choice of a different professional path, even though this diminished her wealth and status, in order to give herself the opportunity to fulfil her creative ambitions. She might not have made it as an artist anyway, and caring for her parents impinged only to some degree on her working life. But the paradoxical outcome for Nora is that, in partly obeying her mother's injunction, she never gets an opportunity to manage any childcare responsibilities of her own. The power of the novel is its exploration of this piercing irony.

6

Explaining the Paula Principle

Factor three — self-confidence and identity

Some famous actors throw up due to nerves before a first performance, but that doesn't stop them getting wholeheartedly into their character and wowing the audience. Some 'ordinary' people rise high up the ranks because they have enormous self-confidence, and this makes others believe in them, too; by contrast, some individuals are highly talented yet never believe in themselves enough to allow their talent to blossom. Then there are those who seem to live their professional and personal lives in compartments: sure of themselves to the point of arrogance in their work, uncertain and indecisive at home — or vice versa.

Self-confidence is a curiously streaky characteristic, which can be both obvious and indefinable. Gaining it, or losing it, can have dramatic effects. Anyone who works in adult education, as I have for most of my life, will know that the most common — and heartening — outcome for adult learners is an increase in their self-confidence. It is extraordinary how often people have felt undermined by their early education to the point where they fundamentally doubt their capabilities, and yet if they can be tempted back into learning, it has a transformative effect. We've seen that with the fictional Rita and the very real Geordie women in Chapter 3. A little learning may be said to be a dangerous thing, but for adults even a very little learning of almost any kind can positively transform their view of themselves.

While there's a strong link between education and belief in oneself, there's no guarantee that one leads to the other. For all their educational success, women often lack self-confidence in ways that inhibit them from applying for the next step up ('I don't think I could quite manage it'), or even from considering it ('Me go for that job — you must be joking!'). It's crucially important to stress that this happens at every level: from women with fairly low-level qualifications who will not take the first step up, to those who have already achieved much and appear to have had all the success needed to give them confidence, yet waver at the next step. It happens to men as well, but not at all to the same degree. Many more men than women are happy to go for a job for which they may be only partly, if at all, competent or qualified. That is, after all, one reason for the Peter Principle.

The commonsense evidence on this is overwhelming. From her experience as a trade-union representative in many different Midlands workplaces, Wilma said: 'If there's a job to apply for, women will list all the requirements and think whether they can fulfil each of them, whereas men will just say, "Oh, I can do that" — they've got more willingness to, ah, blag their way through.'

Ann Oakley has been pondering these issues since she wrote her pioneering book, *The Sociology of Housework*, over 40 years ago.[1] 'I come back the whole time to this question of self-confidence, why men have so much and women so little,' she told me when I asked why she thought that men grow up with more confidence in their own abilities. 'In the end, one can only speculate. But women are brought up to think about other people as much as or more than themselves, whereas men are brought up to think of themselves as autonomous separate individuals with their own path. [For women] it's more difficult to be selfish.' She told me about a book called *Towards a New*

Psychology of Women, written in the 1970s by psychologist Jean Baker Miller. 'A chapter in that was called "Doing Good and Feeling Bad", and that influenced me a lot in the way I thought about power relations.'

PP factor three, self-confidence and identity, accounted for 23% of website votes as to the cause of the Paula Principle. Let's look at why.

The 60/20 confidence–competence axiom

Lack of confidence as a barrier to achievement at work is not unique to women; there are many men who experience it in ways that can cripple their careers and their chances of fulfilment at work. But it arguably has a stronger and more pervasive effect on women. Here are some of the ways it seems to work:

- Women are more likely not even to entertain the notion that they have a potential career, in anything.
- Where they do envisage a career, they may set their sights lower than do men with equivalent competences.
- When it comes to specific steps upwards, such as applying for jobs, women are more hesitant, and more likely to consider that they cannot do the job in question.
- At work, women are less likely to claim the credit for their contribution, or to argue for their potential contribution.
- Women may not accumulate confidence so rapidly as a result of success, so that, even when they rise well up a career ladder, they still may not believe in their abilities.

Who can testify to this, beyond individual women themselves? There are many academic studies,[2] but recruitment specialists are a particularly fertile and compelling source, working either as 'human resource' staff within organisations, or in agencies that find and channel women and men towards appropriate jobs. My conversations with people in these positions produced a high consensus that men put themselves forward far more often for jobs, and for jobs for which they are only partially qualified.

David Fielding handles recruitment for senior posts in public and private sectors and has taken a particular interest in putting women forward as candidates. 'Women will be more likely to draw attention to the three things they can't do,' he says briskly. 'I'm always getting evidence that women underestimate what they can do. I got all my team together to look at people we'd recruited onto shortlists and there was a very clear pattern.' Women, he said, claim less for themselves than they might do, and than men do.

The consensus, from my interviewees and from recruitment specialists, was so clear that it leads me to offer the *60/20 confidence–competence axiom*: men will consider themselves qualified for a job if they reckon they can do at least 60% of it; women will disqualify themselves if they believe there is 20% of the job that they *can't* do. Others may calculate the percentages differently, but there's no doubting the axiom's validity.[3] A recent book entitled *The Confidence Code* sets out the evidence in detail. The authors include strong advice on how women can turn thought into action, for example by learning to take risks more, and harbour criticisms less.[4]

There's a danger here. Some women object quite strongly to including self-confidence as a PP factor, on the grounds that it suggests that the fault lies with women. The implication is that, if only women had more confidence, there wouldn't be a problem, thus loading responsibility for lack of progress at work back onto women. Lesley, a former professional in the not-for-profit sector, put it this way: 'Here's a weird thing. There's something wrong about the system and yet the way to fix it is to make ourselves fit into the system rather than to make the system better reflect who we are.' Now a policy adviser on work and welfare, she goes to a lot of think-tank discussions: 'At some points I have thought, *I'm not being taken seriously in this debate*, and

I find it hard to sort out whether that was a gender thing or because I hadn't done economics, or was it a confidence thing ... the closer you get to economics, the fewer women are there.'

One male reviewer of *The Confidence Code*, US cultural commentator David Brooks, also expressed doubts:

> It's interesting to read the evidence as a guy, especially if you're a self-aggrandizing pundit who covers politics and public life. I almost never see problems caused by under-confidence, but I see (and create) problems related to over-confidence every day ... So my first reaction when reading of female under-confidence is not simply that this is a problem. It's to ask, how can we inject more of this self-doubt and self-policing into the wider culture. How can each of us get a better mixture of 'female' self-doubt and 'male' self-assertion?[5]

His comment resonates strongly with me.

Even when a woman is doing a job perfectly competently, to everyone's satisfaction, she may suffer from 'imposter syndrome', the feeling of just waiting to be caught out as manifestly incompetent after all. There's a complex interaction between realistic appraisal of one's limitations on the one hand and unnecessary lack of self-belief on the other. Cutting across this personal angle is the set of external factors that push women into losing self-belief, or never acquiring it in the first place.

Wilma makes the point directly: 'I'm nervous about the confidence thing. It's absolutely right, and there's none of us here that wouldn't say that confidence gets in the way of women's careers. We surveyed our 27,000 members — the majority of whom are women — and confidence was the number-one factor stopping them taking the next step. What I'm nervous about is this: that we build into the research that the women can't do it.'

The confidence trap: Borgen and the imposter syndrome

The TV series *Borgen* is a rich source of material for the Paula Principle. Its principal character, Birgitte Nyborg, is leader of the Moderate Party going into the Danish elections. She is married to an economics lecturer, with two school-age children, and one recurrent theme is her struggle to get home in time to see the children (and her husband). On the eve of the election, the candidates all appear in a televised debate. Birgitte suddenly discards her spin doctor's text and speaks from the heart, beginning with the admission that she could not get into her dress because she had put on weight. 'We are who we are,' she says, 'and must live up to our mistakes.' She goes on to give a barnstorming speech about inequalities. This propels her party to a big success in the elections.

The day after the election, Bent, her trusty and experienced adviser, tells her that her party is just waiting for her to take them on to a prominent position in the new coalition: 'Now go in there and thank them — and lead them,' he says as they walk down the corridor on their way to a triumphant party reception. Birgitte stiffens and says, to herself more than to Bent: 'But what if I don't know how to do it?' She then walks in to greet her cheering supporters.

Katherine, whose career was in social research, agrees with the importance of confidence as a factor, but distinguishes two different categories: the individual level, where people do not feel confident in themselves, and the social level, where the lack of role models makes the decision to go for a particular position more difficult. This seems a useful distinction, though in practice the two are not separate. Many individuals, with women disproportionately among them, do lack confidence, and this inhibits them from going for jobs or promotion that anyone looking in from the outside could tell they are perfectly able to manage. This is why mentoring and other forms of support are so important for encouraging women to reach further than they would have, left to themselves, and to take proper credit for their own competences. On the other hand, there are wider influences that undermine that confidence: absence of role models is one, but there are many others, such as the behaviour of bosses or colleagues.

This is a clear case where two PP factors overlap and interact: self-confidence and discrimination. What might look like a lack of self-confidence can be a response to circumstances which lead a woman, quite reasonably, to conclude that her chances are low. Some of this may be driven by concerns which are quite peripheral to the job itself. A woman might not want to put herself forward because she does not think she can handle the kind of social interaction that seems to be a part of the job, even though it doesn't figure anywhere in the job description.

There are also forms of what might be called cultural discrimination: off-putting practices that have nothing to do with the intrinsic nature of the job, but that serve to deter very many women from applying. In the British and Australian contexts, we need look no further than the House of Commons and the House of Representatives for a vivid example of the tension between personal attributes and the nature of the job — in this case, the job of being a political representative. Prime Minister's Questions and its Australian counterpart, Question Time, are parliamentary knockabouts that demand quick thinking but also seem to require a lot of shouting and, above all, a willingness to use any opportunity to rub your opponent's nose(s) in whatever metaphorical dirt comes to hand.

On the positive side, PMQs and Question Time do provide a degree of accountability, obliging the Prime Minister to appear regularly to answer questions in a way that never happens in most countries. But the form it takes embodies a grotesquely distorted image of how democratic politics should be conducted — one that infects much other parliamentary behaviour. The media, of course, love the theatre of it. But it puts women at a disadvantage, because often they cannot shout as loudly as men, and mostly do not want to. And it turns many off, not just from aspiring to be prime minister but also from politics altogether. Is an ability to perform in the style epitomised by this type of parliamentary session a necessary characteristic of political representatives? Should jeering be in the skill set required? It's doubtful. At the last UK general election, I listened to a youngish Bengali woman who was standing as a parliamentary candidate reflect on this dilemma in a panel debate at a local college: 'When you watch it, you think, do I really want to get into this?' she admitted to the audience. 'Is this where I belong?' She was elected.

It's not easy to draw the boundary around where confidence stops and self-promotion starts. Nicola has expended an enormous amount of energy on political causes, almost all in a voluntary capacity. She has been very involved in promoting the cause of greater female representation, and has tried several times to become a parliamentary candidate herself. A big part of her work has been in developing women's willingness to put themselves forward, and their confidence in areas such as public speaking. Nicola said: 'You don't actually have to be confident, you just have to look as if you're holding it together. What matters is that you sound as if you're absolutely sure. If you're someone like me, who says, "But couldn't we do it like this ..."', it sounds as if you don't know what you are doing.'

I interviewed her together with her daughter Frances, who is in her late 20s, works in the voluntary sector, and is equally committed politically. Frances sees change coming, as women come to recognise their own competences. 'As women's education improves, are they not going to be savvy, and choose not to do the low-paying jobs where they are disrespected? I applied for a job and was eminently qualified, but I wasn't shortlisted, so I asked for feedback. [As a result] I've got better at selling myself.'

But she recognises the tensions around self-promotion: should women aim to become better at putting themselves forward, or is this to address things from the wrong end?

'I've got a real problem with the Equality Commission [her current employer] because they are saying, "If you're able to sell yourself, then it's okay" — this is the Equality Commission! My development has come through battering my head against brick walls. I'm incredibly determined, but I get to the point where I say, "For fuck's sake, why am I bothering?"'

I found it a piquant irony that, later on in the conversation, Frances repeatedly urged her mother to stand in the upcoming mayoral elections in her home city — but without managing to get her to change her mind.

Olivia works in a very different context — international marketing. The business is all about promoting things and people. But how far does this extend into the behaviour of the staff themselves? 'I've been told in my last review to be more extrovert, which I thought was really inappropriate. They opened with, "This is a really good review, your work is really great," but then they went on to talk about the fact that I'm quiet and have a lack of identity in the office. They said, "Why are you like that?" I was really taken aback, and was unsure how to respond. It felt like a character assassination, and completely unrelated to what we were meant to be discussing!'

Her reviewers were a man and a woman, so it was not just a question of male perceptions. 'A couple of days after my review I brought it up with them and told them that it felt like they were asking me to change my personality,' she told me. 'They said, "No, no, it's nothing like that." I thought, I may be quiet but I already have an identity.'

She resolved the issue, but it left a mark.

Unprompted, Olivia confirmed exactly the mindset that generates the 60/20 axiom: 'It's not that I don't go for promotions, but I don't put myself forward for other things in the agency. If I think about looking for other roles, and jobs in other agencies, I definitely think, *I've got to be able to do everything on that job spec*, whereas other people — men — will just say, "If I can do three of the five things then I'll manage my way through."'

Soleine has every reason to ooze confidence. She has an international educational background, having graduated from the elite Parisian college Sciences Politiques with a degree that included a final year at a US Ivy League university, and then completing a double Masters in Finance and International Political Economy at the Paris Institute of Political Studies and the London School of Economics. She went straight into management consultancy, working for four years for the Boston Consulting Group, first in Paris and then in London. Soleine has published a novel, *Carrières à ciel ouvert,* which effectively (and readably) captures her own experience and that of 30 peers from her high-flyer generation.[6] We spoke on Skype, Soleine having recently moved to East Africa to work in global health.

She tells me that she and her peers might have received a prestigious education, but they were utterly unprepared for 'what is probably the biggest change in your life since entering school for the first time'. The institutions that equipped them with the high-level professional skills to get a world-class first job do relatively little to prepare them for the actual experience. 'I do subscribe to the confidence gap,' she says. 'In consulting, when you participate in a top executives' meeting, very often you're the only woman round the table, even in, say, a cosmetics business, and you can't help noticing that. I also think women tend to find it more difficult not to take setbacks personally. Since I started working, I've seen several female colleagues cry, and have cried myself, due to work. And though some men acknowledged to me when I was doing interviews for my book that they had found this period [the entry into a career] difficult ... somehow that didn't seem to lead to the same symptoms.'

From being at the same high level as her peers at university, Soleine found herself in her first job at the bottom of the hierarchy at work, the most inexperienced person in the company: 'As such, you may be given quite menial jobs and treated in a slightly condescending way. Your confidence levels go right down; your whole identity is at stake. Feedback can be brutal.'

Of course, this is the case for males, too. But, whereas most men may be able to compartmentalise their feelings more and/or drown their sorrows at the bar, women tend to take it all more personally.

'In big companies,' Soleine continued, 'everything is quantified. In consulting, for instance, to help you "improve" quicker, you're evaluated with a set of 20-plus criteria every few weeks, and this can make you feel *objectified* — it is you as a person who is being judged, not just your professional competences. You know, if you are told, say, that your communication or your analytical capabilities are not good — that's not just about your work, that's about you.'

We're back to how competence is defined and recognised. That very basic value question occurs again and again, almost irrespective of pay levels. If this can happen to someone as highly qualified and high-earning as Soleine, others lower down are likely to be side-swiped by far less bruising experiences of a similar kind.

The silence around women's work

One reason that Soleine decided to write her book was that she couldn't find any other women's experiences to relate to, whether through real life, books, or films, to help her when she was struggling.

'I thought that entering the workplace was a really challenging time, especially my first year,' she tells me. 'With time, I felt more ready to open up about these difficulties I had experienced, and that meant that others could open up to me about theirs, leaving pride aside. And that showed me that it wasn't just me and it wasn't just consulting, but more of a generalised phenomenon.

'When you enter your professional life, it's so new and it takes a huge space in your mind. You need to be able to control it, to shrink it a bit, so you can exist as an individual again. But when I looked at literature, I found that there is an absence of public accounts of the experience of work, and especially of the initial spell in a career. There are some exceptions — *Bel Ami*, for example, by de Maupassant, tells the story of a young man who becomes a journalist, but that's in the 19th century, and not really a useful role model today!'

This echoes exactly my experience in looking for fictional illustration for the Paula Principle generally. I asked friends who are considerably better read than I am to point me to examples from literature. They included members of a quite large women-only book group, many of whom are professionally or semi-professionally involved in literature of different kinds. They nearly always directed me to women writers from the past, such as George Eliot or Jane Austen. So I went to the British Library to investigate further. I consulted several encyclopaedias, first of women writers, and then of fiction more generally — about ten volumes in all. It was hardly what you'd call rigorous research, but in none of the indexes did 'work', 'employment', 'job', or 'economic' figure at all in relation to women. The nearest I could get were five entries in Paul and June Schlueter's *Encyclopedia of British Women Writers*, under 'Women and Feminism: equality in the workplace'. Of these, two were from the 19th century (Anna Brownell Jameson and Charlotte Turner Smith), and the other three from the first part of the 20th century

(Olive Schreiner, Mary Amelia St Clair — aka May Sinclair — and Beatrice Webb).

There is the Bechdel test, which assesses any work of fiction, film, or book, by one criterion: do two female characters ever talk about anything other than men?[7] (The test was named after American cartoonist Alison Bechdel, who had one of her characters come up with the idea.) Apparently over half of all movies, including Academy Awards movies, do not pass the test.

I'M NOT MOTHERING YOU, PATRICK! I'M PATRONISING YOU.

As Soleine observes: 'So much for any in-depth conversation of professional issues! That's why I think it would be so helpful to have more documentation on this time of your life — you could learn that it's quite normal to be in the kind of position I was in and to get that kind of feedback ... As I see it right now, being a young professional and a woman is a bit like being in a swimming pool. You're in your lane, and you don't really know what's happening outside in the next lanes. It's a bit blurry, and you feel lonely. So, if we can get more evidence and stories, you can see what's happening to the people swimming in the lanes next to you.'

It's truly surprising that there is not a wider range of fictional experience to draw on, given what an important factor the workplace is in many women's lives.

Confidence and identity

Economists like to give all individual skills and qualifications a label: 'human capital'. I've used the term a few times myself in this book. It signals that competences can be seen as a form of investment, in the same sense as any investment of cash. This perspective is behind the whole Paula argument, which simply asks why the returns are higher for men's skills than for women's. Not everyone likes this metaphor, but we can usefully extend it to cover the issue of self-confidence, and talk about *identity capital*. Our identity capital is our degree of a secure sense of ourselves as we engage in all kinds of transactions and negotiations. It is closely linked to self-esteem. The phrase was coined by Canadian social psychologist James Côté, who was particularly concerned with young people's sense of identity, and how they securely negotiate their transition into adult life,[8] but it applies perfectly well across all ages and stages of life, and perhaps especially to women.

Being low on identity capital can be as hard as being without any qualifications. It is often linked to lack of educational success. My colleagues and I saw many examples in a study we made a decade ago of the benefits of adult learning. Doris was someone whose experience of rediscovering her identity though adult education after a period of intensive childcare was shared by many other mothers with small children. She said: '[In class] I'm just a person. I'm not somebody's mum. And that's what I've learnt — I used to be just there for everybody else. Then suddenly it's like, "You've got a name."'[9]

The need to have a name was just one aspect of what several mothers told us about the extraordinarily powerful effect education can have in restoring a sense of adult identity. It's a further step, and often a long one, to get back into a job or onto an upward career path.

In short, education can enhance self-confidence as well as skills, at any age or stage. But the simple proposition here is that, insofar as women lack identity capital, they will not be able to put their human capital to effective use. It's no good having a good college record, a fistful of technical qualifications, or even a couple of doctorates if you simply have no confidence in your own ability to cut it in the working world. The poor match between levels of human capital and identity capital is readily recognisable as part of the explanation for why women do not realise the full potential of their competences.

Confidence not only depends on your own sense of self but also on how behaviour is seen and interpreted by others. This is how Jo, a female architect, explains the shortage of women in architecture (a shortage that might seem surprising, given the profession's strong aesthetic orientation): 'In architecture, you need to make mistakes — it's inevitable. And women worry about making mistakes.' But the consequences of error are different for the two sexes. I listened to a highly experienced and senior female human resources manager in a large corporation make this trenchant observation to a parliamentary committee: 'When a woman fails, the burden of her failure is borne by all women in the organisation. When a man fails, it's just a "bad hire".'

Tricia Hartley has run the Campaign for Learning for many years. She described to me some of the Campaign's research, which showed that women are much more reluctant than men to claim expertise — the 60/20 confidence–competence axiom again. Once the word 'expertise' was replaced in their survey forms by the word 'experience', women became far readier to see themselves as fully competent people. The higher status implied by the word 'expertise' seemed to them to be beyond their grasp. It is true that expertise and experience are not the same thing, but the women's unreadiness to claim the former is telling.

This reticence to claim what is theirs extends to pay.[10] A male vice-chancellor confided mournfully to me that efforts to reduce the gender pay gap in his university were undermined by the reluctance of female economists in his business school to negotiate for higher pay. His similarly qualified male economists showed no such reticence. This affected the whole university's equality profile: business school salaries weigh heavily in the overall picture, and the progress his institution had made towards greater equality in many other disciplines was totally overshadowed by the results from this single school. Whether it's applying for salary rises, promotions, or jobs, women can hesitate for the wrong as well as sometimes the right reasons, in spite of encouragement.

These examples are of women who have already succeeded professionally as well as educationally, for instance as architects, managers, or academics. The confidence argument applies much more strongly to those who work at lower levels, and may never have experienced such success. If you have not competed for jobs and won the competition, or levered yourself up a few rungs through other means, you will be less inclined to believe you can make progress. In a study of the barriers to progression faced by the low-paid, one woman described her feelings about interviews as they are now conducted: 'It feels like an interrogation ... You feel sick before you even go, don't you? So if you're the sort of person who can sell yourself, then fine, but if not, then once you're in a job it's easier to stay there.'[11]

I have to reiterate here that I accept that men may also experience lack of self-confidence. There is no simple polarisation, with all men puffed up in one corner and all women wilting in the other. But this does not mean there is anything like symmetry in the distribution of self-belief across the sexes.

Women's lack of self-confidence is a major drag on the pay-off to their educational success. But it's not an unalterable characteristic. Wilma was keen to stress both its importance and the need not to overplay it: 'It's really important for your book that you dwell on the confidence and the lack of confidence. But — if I can say so — you also have to mirror that there are plenty of women out there who are confident, and yet they still don't get on.' She insists that it's never too late for people to raise their sights: 'I've worked with women who've spent 20-odd years as a domestic in a hospital and never done anything else, and then something I've done or that one of our reps has done unblocks something and — whoosh! — she's gone on to something else.'

It is also important to reflect on what confidence is and is not. The standards for what counts as confidence, and where confidence spills over into arrogance, are different for men and women. A woman who speaks her mind at a meeting is often seen as pushy, even aggressive, when exactly the same language or behaviour from a man would be regarded as normal.[12] I'm not trying to make all women out to be Snow White–like figures — strikingly, my union interviewees said that they had to handle more bullying cases in which women, not men, were the bullies — but there's no doubt that, in terms of demeanour, different standards are subconsciously applied.

When it comes to promotions and other internal rewards, there may be a penalty, due to a difference in how women and men present their cases. Frances, working in the voluntary sector, expressed her frustration about this: 'I think women fall by the wayside because they don't have these achievement goals ... apparently I haven't done enough strategic stroking of those I need to stroke in order to get on. I haven't spent enough time telling my boss what great things I've done. In fact, I don't even know what it is that I need to do in order to get on.'

For Frances, the reward systems are too narrow: 'What is rewarded is doing the things in your job description — no one cares if you've parked those things to help someone else. No one wanted to mentor me, because they had too much to do achieving their core objectives.'

Measuring one's own value

What will the future look like? I think there are two different perspectives, which may rub awkwardly against each other. Women will come to show greater confidence in their own competences, and be able to assert their rights to equal recognition. At the same time, maybe there will be more questions around how healthy a system is where rewards depend on individuals' willingness to promote their own value aggressively.

I end this chapter with a blog post I wrote in February 2014:

Mrs Moneypenny, a *Financial Times* columnist, wrote this weekend about how depressing she finds it that Mary Barra, the new head of General Motors, is being paid a basic salary of $1.6 million. This is 25% less than her male equivalent at Ford. The gap is a significant one, and not atypical, though I find it hard to get too worked up about discrimination at this level. What I find depressing is Mrs M.'s subsequent argument. Apparently Ms Barra's predecessor at GM is being rehired as a consultant, at $4m (we aren't told if this is an annual fee, but I assume so).

Mrs M. comments: 'That is someone who knows his value and negotiates well. That might be the role model I would want my non-existent daughters to look at.'

I'd take a rather different line. Ms Barra's predecessor looks to me like someone who is well in with a group, presumably heavily male and certainly all wedded to very high remuneration levels that multiply massive inequalities, who make decisions about financial rewards at GM. The same men probably also sit on remuneration committees for many other large corporations. Markets in any true sense don't come into these decisions much.

I am all in favour of women learning to negotiate for a fair deal for themselves. There is a big distinction, though, between getting a fair deal, and extracting the maximum. 'Value' in this context is not something that is determined by some impersonal process; it involves particular people with particular outlooks and interests making particular decisions.

The key point for me is whether we want our organisations and their remuneration systems to be governed in ways that applaud the kinds of individual behaviour geared to extracting maximum personal reward; and as a result *encourage women to behave like the men who do this most successfully.* We need changes in the reward system, very much so. But I'd rather see movement on this taking a different direction: instead of cheering if more women become like men in procuring (a good term, I think) outlandish salaries and bonuses, we should be asking how we get an overall fairer and less unequal reward system — *because this will benefit far more women.*

I would certainly like my daughters to know their value, and to negotiate well. Indeed, I've just been advising one of them on how and when to ask for a pay rise. But someone who extracts huge sums of money because their position and contacts enable them to do so is not what I think of as an ideal role model. I'd like them to have a really sound idea of what they are worth. This should certainly include relativities — what they are paid compared with their equivalents. But I'd like them to have their own sense of value and worth, against which they can judge what they want to negotiate.

I have no doubt about the significance of the confidence factor. It's a question of what form the confidence takes, and how far it's an individual or a cultural problem. I discuss later whether women should be seeking to take on male patterns of achievement at work, or whether it would be better to aim for reverse convergence, which entails men's work patterns moving closer to those of women. Either way, confidence is a major factor. For, while women will need more 'confidence' if they are ever fully to ape the male style, men need just as much confidence to buck current ideas about what constitutes a respectable career path. Meanwhile, Robert Browning's wonderful incitement to aspiration applies, surely but unevenly, to both sexes: 'Ah, but a man's reach should exceed his grasp, Or what's a heaven for?'[13]

7

Explaining the Paula Principle

Factor four — social capital

We met Olivia in the previous chapter. She has worked in two areas where it is important to be able to project an image, inside the workplace as well as outside: first in television, and then in marketing.

'So many senior people in television are men, and they tend to be more comfortable hanging around with younger men,' she told me. 'I've seen them identify a younger man who they like and get along with, and then make them their go-to person. In this way, it's easier for young men starting out in TV as it's quite easy for them to make friends with influential senior men, and they kind of work their way up that way. So unless you have someone who is a bit of a mentor, it can be quite difficult.'

In her current organisation, a branding consultancy, there was a perception among the women, at least until recently, that it was much easier to get on as a man. 'There was all this "Let's go and have a whisky together" — lots of male bonding going on outside work. There was one particular guy who really spearheaded this kind of thing. In my view, he's a bit of a tragic case: he's a middle-aged guy who is desperately holding on to some kind of youth. But he's now left to run the Sydney office, so that aspect has been minimised. There's not the same sense of there being "in people".'

Olivia's sentiment is echoed by Aisha, who works in the very different context of the civil service: 'They used to have the old boys' club, going out for a drink on Friday afternoons. That was in the old Inland Revenue days, but it still continues. They'll talk about sport, but then get on and talk about work. They're quite secretive about it, you know, they put it in their diaries but don't talk about it. I only know about it because one member happened to tell me about it. They have their own insecurity, in case women hear them speaking in this laddish kind of way — but who cares?'

PP factor four, lack of vertical social networks, or social capital, accounted for 14% of website votes. Let's begin our discussion with a look at social networks.

Same social networks, same old choices

Aisha is one of a group of women I interviewed in Her Majesty's Revenue and Customs. She is an operations analyst in the Central Analysis and Information Unit, and has a background of family entrepreneurialism. She has found not being able to make her mark more quickly quite frustrating. Part of that is a matter of timing: she joined HMRC at the time of the 2007 recession, when jobs were hard to come by and career paths shrinking. But it is also due to what she sees as practices and customs that don't allow her talents to show through and earn their reward. Her male peers seem to be making quicker progress up the ladder, partly, it seems, because it is easier for them to be included in the informal networks through which information flows around the workplace. She may also, of course, be subject to some degree to a different form of discrimination because of her ethnic background.

Most of the HMRC women I spoke to had been there for some time — for one of them, Susan, our interview took place on the day before she was due to leave, after 37 years of service. They all agreed that there had been positive changes in the way women were regarded, but that major barriers were still evident, if hard to pin down precisely. Susan, who was trained in employment law, said: 'I certainly did see a lot of discrimination initially. In fact, when I was in this building for my interview 37 years ago, they asked me how I would cope with having children. I told them that asking this was against the discrimination law. It didn't seem to harm me — in fact, maybe they wanted an assertive woman.'

As she implies, Susan is not one to keep quiet when she has something to say, but she didn't always get heard. 'One manager didn't pay much attention to women. He used not to listen to me. So, after a while I used to stop mid-sentence, just to see if he'd been listening, and he'd just carry on whatever he was doing. One day, I made a suggestion about using a handheld computer, and he talked straight over me, implying it was a stupid suggestion. But about three weeks later, a male member of staff made the same proposal and got a recommendation for it.'[1]

Civil-service departments have to be bureaucratic, in the original sense of the word. They are rule-bound and hierarchical, with a clearly defined structure of grades. The women talked a lot about these grades and how you did or didn't move from one to another. The procedures for promotion had certainly changed over time. In the old days, you couldn't apply for promotion but were selected to be put forward for it. This was on the basis of a personnel report, but it also put great power in the hands of the sponsoring individuals. Susan described the process: 'There was a bit of the old network, or somebody would ring someone else and say have you got anyone — you know, your DI (Divisional Inspector) would ring round, asking if his colleagues had anyone [they wanted to put forward]. If you didn't know people, you wouldn't be encouraged.'

Now you are expected to apply for promotion, which makes success somewhat — but only somewhat — less dependent on having a 'sponsor' to back you up. Susan was not sure how much this had actually helped women, because of the confidence factor. Aisha added: 'You have to go for an interview panel, so it's not just the manager. Now, in one sense that's very good, and fairer. But it means that you've got to be good at interviews, which means if you're good at blagging you're more likely to make an impression. Especially if there's an outsider on the panel. You may have done all your tax duties, but if you can't hit a high level on the day, that's it.'

Having a manager who will push you and back you is crucial. This may be exactly the same for men as well as women, but it was certainly a recurrent theme among many of the women I spoke to in other work environments. A surprising number of them credited powerful support from men above them in the organisation for the progress they had made. Wilma, from Birmingham, affirmed that when she said: 'I tell you, what drove me was a man. When I started in the union movement, he really pushed me. He pushed me and pushed me for six whole years.'

In the HMRC, too, several male managers were credited with playing crucial parts in enabling women to progress. Sandra came to England from the British Guyana in 1984: 'I started at the lowest grade, AA (administrative assistant). Within a year, I was on temporary promotion. I got promoted, got the training, [and was] then promoted to Higher Executive Officer — it took me a while, but I didn't think I was discriminated against; I thought my efforts were valued. Every opportunity has come about through someone else pushing me, saying go for this, do this, do that.'

But it only works so far and no further. 'When I got to HEO, that's when I hit the glass ceiling,' says Sandra. 'I think generally there were times when I would look at other people and think: *How did they get that job?* When you don't come from the same background, there are little things you just don't understand. I don't mean this in a discriminatory way — it's just your cultural upbringing.'

Sandra meant by this, I think, that she did not grow up in England but in a colony. Culture is not just about different countries or races. It is something that runs through organisations, favouring some forms of behaviour and outlook and, therefore, logically, disadvantaging others. This is inevitable — even the most anodyne organisation has a culture of some kind. The Paula question is how equitably a particular culture works in general; and, specifically, how fairly it works in relation to women's competences being recognised.

There are various levels to this. Women are less likely to join male colleagues for a drink after work if they have caring commitments at home. That cannot mean men should not go for a drink and talk sport, and, naturally enough, when they are there also talk about work. Along with the gossip, they might pick up occasional interesting titbits about upcoming opportunities, or just items that are useful to them at work. That's an advantage, but only unfair if the occasion is in effect exclusive; probably all an organisation can do is to make sure that useful information is as widely spread as possible, and that the bonding which such socialising promotes does not unduly favour those 'inside' the circle.

Sometimes cultural effects are much more savage, as Brenda's story illustrates. An Oxford graduate, she began her civil-service career in what was then the Department of Social Security, a spending department making welfare policy. She had a spell managing a social-security office, which administered welfare to an area of London. Returning to a policy role, she transferred from the Department of Social Security to the Treasury. The Treasury's role is to amputate as much as possible from spending departments, and there she encountered a completely different culture from the one to which she had been used. It seemed to her highly individualistic, intellectually and to some extent behaviourally aggressive, with so-called colleagues out to demolish one another's arguments and maybe even more. She found this a difficult adjustment from a very team-based culture.

Given its role, you could make a case for the Treasury, or its equivalent in any other country, to be ideally staffed by sharp-taloned, unempathetic types. Their task is to keep rigorous control of the nation's spending — and so to keep one another up to the mark by drawing departmental blood at regular intervals. It could also be the case that some women take to both of these tasks quite comfortably. Yet the question remains: how well does the overall culture draw on the range of skills and competences available to it? And how is that changing, in the light of the changing profile of qualified people? Brenda makes a general point, relevant not just to her Treasury experience: 'Women are interested in "getting stuff done"; they hate game-playing and internal politicking; they only build networks if they see them as a genuine vehicle for getting things done, and not for the same reason as men do, that is, personal advancement. Their language is about "we", about looking for *complementary skills* in a team, recognising that they themselves cannot do it all. For men, it is about "I"; competitive; their personal career.'

This is a crucial observation. Some skills are testable, in a quite objective way — ability to drive a forklift, for example, or to produce accurate spreadsheets, or even to write an article for a newspaper or an academic journal. But despite all the best efforts of recruitment agencies and HR practitioners, there are often still aspects of any job where being judged competent depends on people whose views on what constitutes competence have been shaped quite directly by what they are used to. What they are used to may match up only approximately with what the job really requires. Is the kind of inclusive, group-oriented approach that Brenda describes in her former role better than or as good as its decisive, competitive counterpart? We can't necessarily tell; what we do know is that, if the way things have been done in the past shapes how people think they ought to be done now, then in many occupations with gender differences that is likely to stack the odds in favour of male ways of doing things, simply because historically men have been the ones doing and deciding.

There are dangers, inevitably, in pushing the distinction between male and female skills too far. Florence, from the BBC, encapsulates that when she says: 'An absolute sexism runs through so many organisations about the divide between what men and women can do. Women are supposed to be good at sorting things out, team players, handholding, but [are] not thought about as being ideas people at all. If you have ideas, you're thought of as opinionated and there-she-goes-again. I think that's ingrained, and it's getting worse with the essentialist ideas of Simon Baron-Cohen and his like. The stereotypes are being reinforced by the new brain science.'[2]

Mary McCarthy's 1963 novel *The Group* offers us a colourful palette of characters, from independent (Polly) to submissive (Kay), baby-focused (Priss) to lesbian (Lakey), and so on. They are introduced to us at Kay's marriage to Harald, an aspiring playwright who turns out to be a drunken philanderer. Before you say, 'Oh, but that was 1963' (when the book was published) or 'That was just 1933' (the period in which it's set), I should point out that my edition of the book has an introduction by Candace Bushnell, author of the successful *Sex and the City*, on which the television series is based. 'Although every generation of women likes to claim ownership of a "new" set of problems that come with being a contemporary woman, *The Group* reminds us that not much has really changed,' Bushnell writes.

The women in *The Group* all intend to work, mostly in publishing, teaching, or medicine — all now feminised professions, as it happens. 'The worst fate, they utterly agreed, would be to become like Mother and Dad, stuffy and frightened. Not one of them, if she could help it, was going to marry a broker or a cold-fish corporation lawyer, like so many of Mother's generation. They would rather be wildly poor and live on salmon wiggle than be forced to marry one of those dull purplish young men of their own set, with a seat on the Exchange and bloodshot eyes, interested only in squash and cockfighting and drinking at the Racquet Club with his cronies.'

The group are Vassar graduates, so they are at the elite end of educated women — high on human capital. (They are also strong on social capital — see below.) But this doesn't get them far. Here is Libby's boss, the not-unsympathetic Mr Leroy, giving her an indication of what she should expect:

> That's another thing, Miss McAusland … Publishing is a man's business. … Name me a woman, outside of Blanche Knopf, who married Alfred, who's come to the top in book publishing. You find them on the fringes, in publicity and advertising. Or you find them copy editing or reading proof. Old maids mostly, with a pencil behind their ear and dyspepsia. We've got a crackerjack here, Miss Chambers, who's been with us twenty years. I think she was Vassar too. Or maybe Bryn Mawr. Vinegary type, with a long thin nose that looks as if it ought to have a drop on the end of it, a buttoned-up sweater, metal-rimmed glasses; a very smart, decent, underpaid, fine woman. Our galley-slave, pardon the pun. No. Publishing's a man's business, unless you marry into it.[3]

Candace Bushnell makes another telling point in her introduction: 'Indeed, in reading the novel, one might wonder if the greatest difference between the women of today and the women of 70 years ago may simply be the word "choices" — a word that lulls us into thinking we have some degree of control over our lives, into thinking even that we have solved "the problem that has no name". In *The Group*, McCarthy's characters have no such out.'

I'm not sure whether Bushnell believes that women now do have greater choice (which is the focus of PP factor five, see Chapter 8) or that this idea is a delusion. I certainly share her admiration for the book.

Social capital

This fourth factor introduces *social capital*, a third form of capital to add to the human and identity capitals we have already discussed. Social capital was first identified in the early 20th century as a crucial component of city life, and given a global profile by the American political scientist Robert Putnam in the 1990s.[4] Putnam argued that social capital — the benefits, economic and otherwise, of cooperation and joint enterprise — is declining in the United States as traditional forms of association wither away; he chose the decline of bowling clubs to symbolise this, suggesting that people now go 'bowling alone', which is also the title of his best-known book.[5] Many disagreed with his actual analysis, but the concept of social capital has taken firm root, in policy thinking as well as in research. The point here is that we need to understand better how being a member of certain networks helps people's careers — and exclusion hinders them. It also brings us back to a fundamental point for understanding the Paula Principle as a whole. Looking at the ways in which human and social capital interact helps us get a firmer grasp on the significance and potential of education (the central component of human capital) in this whole story.

This is a crucial feature of the argument, for the following somewhat heretical reason. The rhetoric around education has become significantly inflated, overselling education as almost a panacea. We're all in favour of education, and we all nod our heads whenever anyone says how important it is. Most of my life has been spent in adult education, so I go along with that. But we can overfreight education; however good, it cannot on its own bring about all the worthy goals that are tacked onto its tail. It is not the royal route to social and economic success. Believing that education is the answer for economic advantage, social mobility, personal fulfilment, and social equality diverts attention from the features of our society and our workplaces that so often frustrate progress towards these worthy goals. The notion of social capital reminds us that, however successfully someone learns, the extent to which they can put that learning to effect depends on a whole number of other factors and processes, including the networks to which they do or do not have access.

A quick breakdown of three types of social capital helps us to understand its relevance.[6] 'Bonding' social capital binds us to people like ourselves; 'bridging' social capital connects us to people we might not naturally associate with, but may come to work with in pursuit of common objectives. Both are useful, and women are lacking in neither of these forms of social capital. The third type, 'linking' social capital, connects us to people above us — not necessarily in our own organisation or occupation, but somewhere higher in the overall structure of power and influence. It is these vertical linking networks that open up career promotions, and to which men have better access.

This is not necessarily a matter of nepotism, corruption, or cronyism. The pervasive impact of this factor is to do with how encouragement is given to pursue a career move: (legitimate) information is passed on, possibilities are informally explored, models of how to achieve are absorbed. Associating with people above you helps you find out what opportunities exist both specifically ('you might be interested in this job that's coming up shortly') and generally, as when you gently absorb the way things are done in a given occupation, without being directly instructed.

All this happens largely implicitly but non-conspiratorially, for the most part openly and perfectly honestly. It will always be the case that people will form these kinds of relationships, tight or loose, however purely meritocratic the system, and that some will gain advantage from them. This, in a competitive labour market, means some others lose as a result. But for the Paula Principle, two general facts combine to give these vertical networks of social capital particular bite: men and women prefer generally to associate with their own sex, and there tend to be more men in the upper occupational levels. The first statement is a constant (see below); the second is changing, but not very fast. The result is a self-reinforcing process that excludes women — imperfectly so, but still powerful in its impact on women's career trajectories. As Paul Seabright says in his provocatively titled *The War of the Sexes*:

> Both men and women display a preference (other things being equal) for networking with members of their own sex. Although unsurprising in itself, this preference has an interesting consequence in organisations where women are under-represented, because networking primarily with their own sex tends to shut women out of networks of power and influence. The result is that while those professional ties that are most instrumentally useful to men are also the ones that coincide with their social ties, women tend to interact with one group of colleagues (largely female) for personal support and a different group (largely male) for professional help, advice, and advancement. [7]

Linking social capital …

Bonding social capital …

Olivia feels well connected, with good mentors, a family with quite good connections, and good female role models in her occupation of marketing. But she noted how segregated the exchanges on work futures can be: 'Certainly the people I have conversations with about careers are my female friends. I have a lot of male friends, but maybe there's a feeling of — maybe solidarity, or maybe more of those conversations are more emotionally fuelled, they're about how you're feeling at work.'

The phrase 'emotionally fuelled' is a telling one: Olivia's female friends will recognise the feelings involved in discussing a career, and so she can feel more secure in talking about it.

Seabright goes on to report that women have as many connections as men do, but they often do not have the right balance of 'strong' and 'weak' ties. Women may be good at networking generally, but there is something of a vicious circle when it comes to rising up the hierarchies. When it comes to careers, men's 'linking' social capital is on average stronger. As I said, this is not mainly about outright nepotism, or unfair favouritism that maybe gets men particular jobs. It is simply the case that at any given level of job it helps to know people who have experience of the levels above, towards which you may be aiming. Knowing them will help you to understand what it involves, and they can support or sponsor your bid for promotion, formally or informally. This is the way of things, even in consciously and conspicuously equitable settings.

On the other hand, the male clubbishness of these elites is indeed a powerful factor in explaining why women so rarely break through to that level. The networks may be formed early (for example, at private school) or in specific settings (such as at golf clubs) that effectively exclude women. How far do women have to adjust in order to fit in with current organisational cultures?

The issue recurs in most, perhaps all, cultures. In one respect, Hyun-Joo is a Korean insider. Both sides of her family have a very strong academic pedigree and career orientation. Her grandfather and her father were both philosophers, the former starting in theology and the latter moving from philosophy and history to become in essence the founder of museum education studies in Korea and an intellectual innovator. Her paternal grandmother was a highly reputed sculptor. Hyun-Joo herself did her first degree at Yonsei University, and then moved to the United Kingdom to do a Masters. Returning to Korea for the first time, she was a part-time lecturer at Yonsei, her alma mater, and was also teaching at other universities, in the classic peripheral position. 'I spent almost all my income on taxis in order to get between the different places where I was teaching. It was very low pay. But this was necessary for me to build up my career.'

Hyun-Joo returned to London, completing postdoctoral research in International Relations at the London School of Economics. She moved back to Korea again, this time to Seoul National University. The SNU faculty in her area had all attended the university to get their first qualifications, and gained their PhDs from the United States. And they were all men. So Hyun-Joo was triply exceptional, as a Yonsei female graduate with a PhD from the United Kingdom.

The profile of the faculty was chauvinist and nationalist. 'We had a faculty meeting. It was held in what we call a "dogs restaurant" [that is, where dog meat is served]. I don't eat meat, and I'm a non-drinker. They all wanted me to drink — hard liquor. I had to walk out. But I'm unusual — other female assistant professors are adjusting to that culture.'

She left soon afterwards, and settled eventually in an academic post in the United Kingdom.

Hyun-Joo was from an established and highly reputed academic family, but did not fit the cultural profile of her institution.[8] I've placed her story in the category of culture and networks. It could, though, be taken to represent discrimination; once again, the PP factors overlap and interact. From a social drink after work to semi-compulsory participation in a dog-meat meal: to a Westerner, these look very different kinds of workplace cultural events. It can be difficult to know how and where to draw the line — if indeed a line can be drawn at all. And they are not all male methods for shutting out women. Lily, one of the county-council employees we met in Chapter 4, referred to the group of women managers in her division as 'the coven', and she was only half-joking.

To repeat, the Paula Principle does not apply only at the more rarified levels of professional groups. Exclusion from networks that count can operate in many different ways, and at all levels. The extent to which women and men are segregated at work, into different occupations or different grades, will naturally affect the range of their networks. The difference is that for women, the effect is more likely to limit their chances of knowing about how to get on professionally. Carers and cashiers have more restricted networks than lawyers or management consultants. But, once again, social class and education are more powerful than gender; in other words, women from middle-class professional backgrounds are far more likely to have useful networks than men from poor backgrounds.

Networks don't always help. Women often support other women, just as men do men, but perhaps more so. As Madeleine Albright, former US secretary of state, once said in testimony to a parliamentary committee on women in the workplace: 'There's a special place in hell reserved for women who don't help other women.' But sometimes being part of a tight-knit set of friends can have a depressing effect on aspirations. Wilma and her fellow trade unionists in Birmingham agreed with one another that on occasion women working at the same level can regard the expressed desire of one of them to move upwards and get a promotion as a kind of betrayal of solidarity: a kind of 'Why would you want to do that?' This is negative social capital, where the sharing of values, which is usually supportive and a source of strength, turns into a force for maintaining the status quo, even at the expense of some of the members' potential personal progress.[9]

The way that networks function brings us back round to the first of our factors. Networks can effectively shut people out without this appearing as overt discrimination, or indeed being designed in any sense as exclusionary. And there are obvious links to the third factor: it takes much more self-confidence to break into a group where you are in an evident minority — or to sustain your sense of identity once you are inside it. It's something that regular insiders find difficult to grasp.

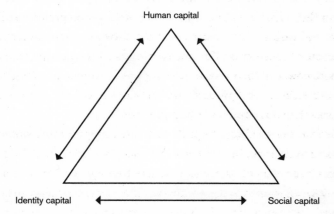

Three Interacting Capitals

Human capital

Identity capital   Social capital

So I close this chapter with an invitation: to use the triangular three-capital framework above to reflect on how the usefulness of human capital (qualifications, skills, competences) is conditioned by the other two forms of capital: identity capital, or the belief in oneself that we explored in the previous chapter, and social capital, or access to helpful networks. Think of some examples, either from your own experience or from that of others, of how these interactions work. Who makes good or poor use of their qualifications? How do the networks function, and why? Then think about how far they play out in different ways for women and men.

I'm not suggesting for one moment that these differences are absolute. But — hard though it is to capture this in organised research — I believe that it is the *interactions* between the three capitals that are critical. In short, women can pile up the competences but, if they don't have decent levels of self-esteem or the right levels of contacts, the pay-off will be low.

8

Explaining the Paula Principle

Factor five — choice

My argument now takes a different turn. The first four PP factors all point to ways in which women are prevented from realising their potential, and their competences are under-rewarded. The underlying argument is that they would rise higher if they were not so hindered. The final reason that so many women do not get jobs at the level they are capable of reaching is diametrically different: it is that they actively choose not to do so, and for good reasons. PP factor five, choice, accounted for 15% of votes on my website as to the underlying cause of the Paula Principle.

I have said that most people would acknowledge the first four factors to be negative features of our society, which we should aim to reduce or remove. True, there are some who believe that discrimination is a thing of the past, or that women's self-confidence needs no reinforcing, thank you very much. Nevertheless, I do think we'd find a reasonable majority, among men as well as women, in favour of doing something about these factors, even though they might not agree on exactly how important or pressing the individual factors are.

When it comes to the fifth PP factor, choice, there will be no such consensus. The notion that women might — and do — actively choose *not* to rise to their competence level prompts some fairly sharp responses, for quite varied reasons. Choice is not just philosophically a slippery concept but also politically a highly charged one, perhaps especially when it comes to gender differences. Not everyone accepts that some women do make such positive choices.

How do we understand choice?

'One has no choice in such matters these days,' said Her Majesty Queen Elizabeth at a royal garden party, to a former Member of Parliament who thanked her over-profusely for ennobling him.[1] I love the putdown, but it also shows how even the most elevated of us have their choices constrained. By contrast, in Act 1 of *Educating Rita*, Rita notes of her husband: 'He wants to take life away from me. I told him I'd only have a baby when I had a choice. But he doesn't understand. He thinks we've got choice because we can go into a pub that sells eight different kinds of lager.' She goes on: 'He thinks we've got choice already: choice between Everton and Liverpool [rival football teams], choosin' which washin' powder, choosin' between one lousy school an' the next, between lousy jobs or the dole, choosin' between Stork an' butter.'

So what looks like choice to one person may not to another, and what seems like choice may in fact be obligation. In thinking about choice, I'm particularly interested in how far Paula chooses her career as it unfolds, and how far these choices reflect her competences.

Below is a list of what I see as simple axioms. The aim is to frame the debate rather than to convince you of a particular position. Some of the reasons for which women choose not to carry on up a conventional career path are positive, but it's a matter of cumulative choice over time, not of individual acts; choosing a career is not the same as picking a pair of socks.

The basic axioms are these.

1. We all make choices almost all the time. Even those who are physically in chains make choices. Only total psychological domination or submission eliminates choice.

2. These choices are constrained by all sorts of factors: external ones, such as when what one ideally wants is simply not available; and internal ones, such as a failure of imagination or depressed aspiration. Both are at play when it comes to women's jobs and careers.

3. There is huge variety in the extent to which people can and do choose. Some of this is to do with material wealth: richer people have more choice. Much of it is to do with intelligence, education, upbringing, experience, and luck. Men have more wealth than women, but are not noticeably favoured in respect of the other attributes.

4. Different cultures, classes, and genders will construe 'choice' and 'choosing' differently (as the quote above from Rita shows). Within each of these categories, people will also vary in how far they see themselves as having choice, and — a separate question — in how far others see them as having choice.

5. It is a mistake to try to understand choice only by reference to individual acts of consumption or decision-making. Most choices, especially women's choices to do with work and family, are shaped by social factors, including other people's preferences and powers.

6. If women say they prefer, for example, to work part-time, or to give priority to family life over a career, it's risky or worse not to accept that they mean it.

I regard these as broadly commonsensical statements. Common sense, of course, is often exactly what needs to be challenged for progress to happen — socially or scientifically — and you as a critical reader may reject some or all of these statements. Still, I hope they provide a useful framework for thinking collectively about this crucial factor.

The choice factor is complex because it is often difficult to draw a clear dividing line between different kinds of choice: between positive choice and all those decisions that are so constrained that it is doubtful whether 'free' choice is truly involved. Yet, however fuzzy it may be, finding some kind of line is crucial. It's a tough challenge: pipe-sucking philosophers, over-rational economists, rat-running psychologists, and many other stereotypical scholars have tackled it, and come away with intellectual bruises to show for it. Can we trust what people say when they tell us, retrospectively, why they chose one course over another? How far can we deduce from their behaviour what they 'really' want? How far are preferences shaped by factors of which people are only dimly conscious? How far are they 'nudgeable', as the emerging branch of behavioural economics has it?[2] It's all getting very complex as science delves further than Freud could ever have dreamt into the mechanisms that shape our behaviour.

However high the bar is set in deciding what counts as 'free' choice, it seems undeniable that women sometimes do choose positively not to go for a position, or for the next level up in what they are doing, or to switch to a better-paying occupation. They do this even though they may be confident that they could do the job (so that PP factor three does not apply), and let's assume that confidence is justified. There are many reasons why they might make such a choice. They may choose lower-paying occupations because they get greater satisfaction from the type of work these occupations offer, such as greater contact with other people or a stronger sense of serving social purpose. Some women prefer to serve talking, responsive human beings rather than to be instantaneously responding to flashing cursors on a financial screen. This is not so very strange. Or they opt to stay at the level they are at rather than assume greater responsibilities — and the hassle and stress that goes with those responsibilities, on top of their responsibilities at home.

Scarlet Harris, women's equality officer at the Trades Union Congress, agrees that the factors all overlap. She makes it clear that, wearing her official hat, she thinks the main ones for women are discrimination and caring responsibilities. Yet for herself she points to choice and says: 'I'd put myself in that category — there are probably jobs I could have got, but I enjoy my job, for the time being, so why should I move? You could flip it on its head, and say why are so many people concerned with going upwards the whole time? Why obsess about going up to be CEO if the job you are doing is fulfilling?'

The headhunter David Fielding makes a similar point, extending it to include some of the reasons why this might be so: 'We have a number of women who just say, "I'm enjoying doing what I'm doing." Implicitly, there are issues about the rewards you get from doing what you do. Having turned around four organisations myself, I'd risk the generalisation that it's more rewarding for men to do something and move on. I'd risk the guess that the longevity of tenure for men as CEOs is shorter than for women. Nurturing people, nurturing top teams, nurturing organisations takes more time and energy than crunching an organisation together, turning things around, and so on.'

Wilma, who, like Scarlet, works in the trade-union movement, said: 'I'll concede the choice thing. I think I've made conscious choices. If you become a manager, your job satisfaction levels might go down, and that for me would be a factor. I've seen management jobs and thought, "Oh, I could do that," but then I wonder what it would mean for my job satisfaction.'

How we choose, and how broad we think our choice range is, are also shaped by the kinds of subject we've studied. Fabienne is a researcher who did a social-science degree at Durham University. Her sociological way of looking at things brings her into conflict with her friends, who come mainly from a natural-science background (even her boyfriend is a biologist). 'I do talk about careers with my friends. My friend Louise is just finishing a PhD in science. All the postdoc jobs there only last two years, so they just have to keep moving around, and that means that women in science just do not progress as fast as men, because they're not as mobile. She just says that it's a choice, and if she wants to be in science, then she has to accept that. I don't see things like that, so we just disagree.'

Deciding what counts as authentic choice is tricky. But introducing choice is also controversial because it risks muddying the issue of fairness. The other four PP factors point to how women are to some extent unfairly denied the material fruits of their educational success. But the choice factor seems, on the face of it, to dilute the impact of that evidence. Women have different preferences and priorities, and earning money comes lower down than quality of the job. On this line of argument, if women choose not to go for promotions or seek other routes upwards, their choices should be respected, and not devalued by implying some kind of false consciousness — in other words, by saying that they don't really know what they want. Some might say, even more sharply, that not to respect women's decisions as being freely made is a patronising way of imposing other (possibly male) values. But I'm well aware, as are many of the women who talked to me, that boosting 'choice' in this sense brings the danger that it simply ratifies existing arrangements. Florence, the radio producer, was blunt about it: 'To say it's free choice is bullshit, really. It's about a capitalist-consumerist kind of choice, and ignores issues of power. If men really wanted to spend their days in playgrounds and wiping toddlers' bums, then they'd do it.'

In any case, are we sure that choice is all it's cracked up to be? In *The Paradox of Choice*, Barry Schwartz suggests that in many areas Western consumers are actually offered excessive choice, which diminishes not only their wellbeing but also their sense of being in control.[3] Once we get beyond a certain number of choices, we suffer, because we always think there might have been a better, or cheaper, option just round the corner if only we'd looked hard enough. The net effect on our wellbeing is negative. Schwartz focuses on consumer goods, but the argument can be broadened to include job choice.

In recent years, choice has risen up the political agenda in the United Kingdom. It has become almost a mantra in the drive to reform public services, such as health and education, under successive governments. The simple — or simplistic — argument is that increased choice will drive up quality and efficiency, as consumers shop around, express their preferences, and put pressure on the providers of these services to improve. Whatever the economic models purport to tell us, the evidence for this effect is very thin. Most people do want their schools, colleges, hospitals, and medical centres to respond to their preferences, but the overriding wish is for a guaranteed level of quality, not for the chance to shop around. They are not only less interested in exercising choice per se, but can also often be uncomfortably stressed about what is entailed in doing so — especially when it comes to services such as health or education, where there is professional expertise involved.

Yet, overall, I'm assuming that enabling people to choose their own patterns and pathways at work is usually a desirable good. Women choosing not to go as far as they might up the career ladder, opting instead for quality of work and a good work–life balance, is surely a positive — provided that they have not been unfairly excluded from any of the options.

Authenticity and the academic path: Molly's story

Molly is a lecturer in her late 30s. We met in the café at
the university where she teaches. Molly had been to a job
interview the previous week for an associate professorship at
a more prestigious university. The post involved responsibility
for part of the teacher education programme. She saw that
the job would take over her professional life, and it simply did
not fit with her own identity as a committed researcher. At
the end of the interview, Molly was asked whether she would
take the job if offered it, and she gave the honest answer: no.
She did not claim that she would have been offered the job,
but this seemed to have been a definite possibility till that
point. 'I know I have to be authentic — in a situation where
I feel right. And I knew it wouldn't be right.'

She had chosen to pass up a possible opportunity to join
a world-class institution. There were also family reasons for
her decision: taking the job would have meant either uprooting
the family or spending at least three nights a week away from
home. These are the kinds of constraints that nibble away at
free choice. But the primary reason Molly gave was one of
'authenticity'; she did not feel that the job would have allowed
her the kind of professional identity she desires. She felt it was
not a position that would enable her to do what she feels right
doing — her particular line of research.

Choice, though, is not about momentary decisions, the
single act of saying yes or no. The process of going for the
job, and getting so close to it, was one that Molly had found
very significant; she called it *validating*. Clearly, anyone should
feel their competences are valued and endorsed if they are
assessed as good enough for such a senior position.[4] I think

there was a further process at work: Molly's *internal validation* of her own judgements and values. It was not that she took pleasure in turning her back on an august institution. She would have placed a high value on working at a research-intensive university. Thus, the validation arose from going through the application and interview process, seeing that she had the competences to do the job (irrespective of whether she would have been offered it) and feeling free enough to make the decision to withdraw because she trusted her own judgement.

The Paula Principle is about competences, and validation is central to competence. That's what all our huge array of examination boards are constantly concerned with — they validate, ceaselessly and expensively. The validation of competences does not have to be formal, although for women this tends to be more important because of their doubts as to whether their competences will otherwise be properly recognised — which is one reason why more women than men put themselves forward for formal training, as we have already seen. It links closely with PP factor three, the need for women to have confidence in their own competences. The most direct, tangible, and consequential form of validation comes from the manager or the employer (current or future): appointment or promotion is a function of competence being recognised. You could even say that *the Paula Principle is fundamentally about validation, internal and external.*

Molly's story of choice started earlier. She had been working with very senior people, notably a female pro-vice-chancellor who came from a business/HR background and who was a significant sponsor, along with a male vice-chancellor, who also supported her. So her 'linking' social capital stock was quite high. The work opened up many options for her to carry on moving up the career ladder; she was on the inside track for managerial positions at senior levels in the university world. But, to the surprise and puzzlement of the senior people who had supported her career, she did not take up any of those options. Instead, she took a cut in pay and in status to go to her current post. 'I think they [her sponsors] were baffled. They were probably looking at me and thinking, "We've given her all these opportunities, why hasn't she taken them?" I'm a competent manager, but there's plenty of others who can do that as well as I can, so for me it's really important to be in a position where I can flourish and do whatever it is that's me. I just love that imaginative journey.'

The pay cut hurt a bit, but not too much. The status drop hurt Molly more. She is what is termed a Lecturer B, which is the upper tier of the basic tenured academic grade. She had to go through the hoops as if she were a probationary lecturer, and had not already been working in the area for many years. Status is linked to power, and the ability to get things done, so her relatively low status (especially compared to her previous trajectory) is a practical constraint. Her story also illustrates how career structures that enable people only to be promoted up a vertical ladder can downgrade the competences of those who choose to do something different.

Why might women choose to stay below their competence level?

In *Rosencrantz and Guildenstern Are Dead*, the Player says: 'We're tragedians, you see. We follow directions — there is no *choice* involved. The bad end unhappily, the good unluckily. That is what tragedy means.'[5]

For some people, especially men, the idea of deliberately not going as far up the occupational ladder as you might is just weird. It is for most of them barely conceivable that anyone who could move up, presumably to greater status and financial reward, should choose not to do so. This is a mindset that has to be confronted if we are to resolve the paradox of the Paula Principle. In choosing not to go as far up the ladder as she could, Paula is by definition foregoing other options. Yet she is making the choice not only as a preferred option but also as one that carries a positive charge.

Let's explore this through the Paula Principle at its most fundamental level: the relationship between competence and reward.

- Paula wants to *carry on exercising the skills she is already using.* She knows she is doing a competent job and wishes to carry on doing it. This is a perfectly rational position, even in rejecting the opportunity for increased financial reward.[6]

- Paula sees herself *doing a job reasonably well but sees scope still to do it better.* Her ambition is to keep learning and improving while doing her same job. This fits well with the stronger tendency of women to see themselves as still needing to learn.

- Paula's potential promotion or new job is at a *higher level but is not actually an attractive job intrinsically.* It may involve a big shift in the tasks involved, a change of environment or social circle, and/or an abandonment of activities that are cherished. A managerial role within a university, for example, is qualitatively different from doing exciting research or inspiring teaching. It may pay more but reward less.

- Paula may be keen on new challenges, willing to move beyond her current position and function — and yet *prefer to move sideways rather than upwards*. Movement need not be vertical to be experienced as a progression. Applying one's skills in a different environment is a positive step, maybe as much as moving to higher responsibilities, as Wilma's story (on page 181) shows us.

Drusilla has had a long career in adult education, often focused on opportunities for women, but when we met she talked mainly about her adult daughter rather than herself. She has come to terms with the younger generation's change in focus, away from seeking equality in professional careers. Her daughter's friends are choosing not to commit themselves to work in the same way as she and her own peers did: 'It's not that they are not aware of structural inequalities, but their solutions are slightly different to those of my generation of second-wave feminism, and how that discourse got kind of appropriated by the Shirley Conran *Superwoman* idea. They look at that and think they can't be doing that. They have seen us struggling to cope with doing it all … I have three young women living with me: my niece, who's 26; my older daughter, who is 22; and my younger one, 19. Their eyes used to glaze over when I talked about this stuff, but now we have discussions on it. They do understand the issues that drove us into second-wave feminism, but they want to go past it, and I feel quite comfortable with that. They are ambitious, but not individually ambitious, not in the same way. They say things like they don't want to be tired; they don't want to work at weekends. They are quite prepared to make choices about not following traditional career routes if that means they have time to do other things that matter to them.'

There's an elephant in the room here: money. Isn't it the case that women who are able to make these kinds of choices are being supported by a partner or family? Or else they tend to be the lesser earner in a dual-earner household, and so don't have the same need to maximise their own earnings? Sometimes, yes. But this all depends on how we go about valuing activities. There is, just possibly, a general mood shift here in attitudes as to what counts as valuable. This shift is not some kind of vague countercultural hand-waving. We are seeing very rigorous measurement techniques applied to a broader range of outcomes than just income. Hard-headed economists and eminent social scientists are doing serious work on changing the way we calculate national progress. They aim to replace 'gross national product' with more socially resonant measures that capture personal wellbeing and environmental sustainability.[7] This means encouraging individuals to look beyond maximising their income and think more about the quality of their working life.

Of course, it's nearly impossible for poorer families, whose choices are by definition limited. But above a certain income threshold, the option is often there for people to follow a track that is not just income-maximising, and there are enough cases to show that the threshold need not be very high. In other words, it's wrong to think that a positive decision not to carry on up the ladder is open only to the economically very comfortable.

Annabel, working-class and of Irish extraction, has been working as a healthcare assistant for 23 years, and for all that time on the same grade. She was 36 when she went back into education, encouraged by a late diagnosis of dyslexia that raised her expectations of herself. She ended up with a degree — and, like the fictional Rita, a divorce, leaving her a single parent with three kids. Has this led to any career advancement? Not in the conventional sense, since she is still in the same position, and is paid at a very meagre hourly rate of £8. She could badly do with more money, and it has been a struggle bringing up the three children on such a basic wage. She could almost certainly have progressed upwards, but that would have meant losing contact with patients and not doing what she is passionate about. Her degree has broadened her outlook and her options, but she has chosen to keep the same pay cheque.

Of course, men also make choices not to go up to the next rung. Wilma supplies an example: 'I have a 34-year-old colleague who is fabulous at what he does, and he never applies to be a project manager, which is the next step up. He's quite frank about why: he likes being a big fish in a small pool. He likes where he is in the food chain of the workplace.' It's an interesting image, which many women might be happy to apply to themselves too.

Georgina, a senior researcher in a middle-sized charity, has a husband who works as a manager in the car industry, and who is clearly an unusual man in that context: 'When we got married, he knew that I was the career person and he decided he would never make a decision that would hold me back from that. He has been incredibly consistent on that, and has prioritised family and children. So there are choices that we make together, and then there are choices that he makes which mean that I can make choices.' Choice, then, is not always a solo activity.

Choosing paid (or unpaid) work

I've not discussed making the positive choice to do the unpaid work of rearing children and maintaining a household, because the Paula Principle doesn't apply to how competences are or are not put to use in this private domain in the same way as it applies to the workplace. But domestic arrangements are nearly always a factor in career decisions. Here are two brief, strikingly contrasted, perspectives.

The first comes from Simone de Beauvoir, in her extraordinarily pioneering *Second Sex*: 'Marriage is the sole career for women. Men have 36 options, women one only — the zero, as in the casino [roulette].'[8] With this striking image, she brings together the notion of marriage as a career (in which the woman may choose to deploy her skills), the sense of the gamble involved (in marriage, obviously, but also in work), and the inequalities between men and women.

Compare this with the contemporary observation of Teresia, a Swedish woman with two children at primary school, who moved to the United Kingdom in 2000 with her British husband. Although she has started her own business, she gave up her original career to raise her family. Interviewed by Rebecca Asher for her book *Shattered*, Teresia says that this decision would have been considered unacceptable in Sweden. 'What's happened there in the last 15 years is that the woman is now just expected to go back to work full-time after a year or 18 months. No one stays at home. I mean, there would be headlines: "This woman has chosen to be a housewife: outrageous!"'[9] As she expresses it, Sweden has removed almost all the structural constraints on women's employment, and added to these strong normative constraints — against her not doing paid work.

Hazel Rowley's fascinating account of de Beauvoir's personal and philosophical relationship with Jean-Paul Sartre summarises her position on the nature of women's freedom:

> Her premise was that the ultimate goal of any responsible human subject should be 'sovereignty'. But this was complicated. If a woman was not free, it could be for two reasons. Her lack of freedom could be *inflicted*, in which case it constituted oppression. Or it could be *chosen*, in which case it represented a moral fault. In both cases it was *an absolute evil*. [my emphasis][10]

De Beauvoir's division into oppression and fault sets two key viewpoints in polar opposition to each other: that lack of freedom is the result of external forces on the one hand, or of personal fibre on the other. I'm groping towards something a bit less binary than de Beauvoir's Cartesian rigour, towards the ways in which several different impulses and desires interact in shaping our behaviour.

Another philosopher, Martha Nussbaum, sees the need for 'a critical scrutiny of preference and desire that would reveal the many ways in which *habit, fear, low expectations and unjust background conditions* deform people's choices and even their wishes for their own lives.' [my emphasis] [11] That begins to unpack the components of decision-making, and to make sure that the social context is properly recognised. In other words, to understand why people express the preferences that they do, we need to understand the kinds of deep-rooted tendencies and tastes that they have often harboured for a very long time (not all of them detrimental). Nussbaum's statement also poses a formidable methodological challenge: how to uncover the ways in which people deceive themselves into believing that they are getting what they want.

The sociologist Catherine Hakim approaches the issue of choice from a very different angle. Her 'preference theory' proposes that women fall into three distinct groups when it comes to mixing work and family. The work-committed give preference to their careers, and Hakim says roughly 20% of women fall into this category. At the other end is a similar proportion of family-oriented women. In between are the 'adaptive' women, about 60% of the total, who blend both commitments. Hakim's controversial stance is that women in most Western countries have reached a position where they have genuine freedom of choice, and these proportions, in how they exercise it, are more or less fixed. She is quite uncompromising: 'There are no major constraints limiting choice', and, 'Affluent and liberal modern societies provide opportunities for diverse lifestyle preferences to be fully realised.'[12]

I find Hakim's conclusions simply unrealistic, and concur with the critique articulated by several commentators on her theory.[13] There is a continuum of preferences, shaped (and reshaped) by a variety of forces, rather than a set of fixed categories. This means, in the Paula Principle context, understanding better the ways women make choices about careers and family lives both willingly and unwillingly — often at the same time. The big mistake, it seems to me, is to have only a single mode of understanding choice. Hakim is right to say that women in most Western countries have more choice than ever before, but wrong to suggest that the choices they make embody fully the preferences they do *and might have*.

Choosing where to work

Occupational segregation means that women and men are concentrated into different job areas. Men march into finance and engineering; women stream into health and school teaching. We've already seen that this is relevant, since female-dominated occupations tend to pay less.

Surely women and men should be able to choose which occupation they work in (provided, of course, they are capable of performing the work), without being cramped in their choice by stereotypes or a lack of substantive freedom.[14] But here is an interesting and significant paradox. Scandinavian countries rank very highly among those where most progress has been made towards reducing gender discrimination. They provide affordable and high-quality childcare, promote parental leave for both sexes, and take a range of positive measures to encourage women into careers. There is a conscious cultural commitment to fostering gender equality. If anywhere, these are the countries where women might be thought to have the freedom to choose where they want to work. So where do they choose to work? Overwhelmingly in health, education, and personal services — exactly the stereotypically feminine areas from which their culture seeks to steer more of them away. The rather surprising picture is that Scandinavian women have a higher level of this 'horizontal' gender segregation than countries with a more traditional view of women, such as Italy and Japan.[15]

Part of the explanation is simple: pay inequality is very low in Scandinavia. Going into teaching or nursing rather than accountancy or banking carries a much lower financial penalty than it does in other countries, especially the United States and the United Kingdom. At the same time, the public sector provides more-flexible working schedules that better suit women, who still take more of the responsibility for childcare — and the public sector is where you find most of the education and health jobs.[16] For most women, the preference does appear to be to go for jobs that have to do with people, rather than with blips on a screen, however fertile the latter may be in salaries and bonuses. Nevertheless, it's striking that a strongly gender-egalitarian culture goes along with a high level of occupational segregation that concentrates men and women quite heavily in different fields. I wonder how our diagram showing the weightings of the PP factors would be completed by Swedes or Norwegians — especially how much weight they would give to choice.

Choices and trade-offs

So the Scandinavian countries combine high rates of occupational segregation with relatively low inequality of pay. Is the former a price worth paying for the latter? Recent research adds a further, major twist to this debate. Looking across some 30 countries, sociologists Jennifer Jarman, Robert Blackburn, and Girts Racko show, first, that there is always a gender pay gap, except for some reason in Slovenia. (All these countries conform to the pattern of competence crossover — that is, women have overtaken men educationally.) In more occupationally segregated societies, such as Sweden, the pay gap is lower and women find it easier to get to senior positions. But the researchers also conclude — looking now at just 12 of these countries — that women are now actually ahead when it comes to the social status or attractiveness of the jobs they hold. Overall, men are more concentrated in manual jobs, sometimes performed in difficult physical conditions, whereas over the years more women have moved into non-manual occupations, out of factories and into offices. Moreover, women have benefitted more than men from the professionalisation of their work, able to move into jobs that are recognised as having professional status. Contrast lorry driver and nurse, builder and teaching assistant. The former are certainly more likely to earn more. But in all 12 countries, apart from Austria, the occupations in which more women work than men tend to be those held in higher regard by society. All this is on average, of course; the top jobs in those occupations still tend to be filled by men, but enough women hold middle-ranking jobs to put them ahead overall in the status stakes.

There is also some recent evidence from Europe that women — again, on average — rate the quality of their jobs more highly than men do. On a 100-point scale, women's satisfaction with their jobs comes out at 60.7 for the European Union as a whole, compared with 57.7 for men. The gap in the United Kingdom is significantly wider: 65.0 to 57.9.[17] All this adds a powerful impetus to the choice argument. Choosing a job that brings status and satisfaction at the expense of money is a decision that most people would quite easily accept as rational — whether or not they themselves would make the same choice. It casts the workings of the Paula Principle in a more friendly light, but it doesn't eliminate it.

Choosing a clear boundary

Still, there are many jobs that neither win much recognition nor offer much chance of progression. Cleaning (homes, offices, or streets) and cashiering come to mind. Sometimes decent or even just above-average wages compensate for these negative features. Often, though, these are exactly the jobs that are not well paid. This may not matter too much, if the jobholder knows that they are only going to be doing it for a short while. Shelf-stacking is tolerable as a vacation job or as an interim position while waiting to move on to something else. It's not great as a lifetime occupation.

People in jobs of this kind may have a purely instrumental view of work: as long as it brings in a reasonable wage, it's acceptable. An important aspect of this is the degree of autonomy or control it brings. In the case of a woman with children to look after, this may mean she knows exactly when she will be free to engage with childcare duties. The work does not go home with her, or occupy her outside the paid-for hours. This is, of course, more usual for low-qualified people, who might not have much choice of career in any case, as Lesley attests.

Lesley worked for many years with Gingerbread, an organisation that supports single parents struggling to make ends meet: 'One of the things we found was that people had aspirations to fit their career round their family — that's what they cared about. I felt two things about that. First, why should those two things be incompatible, and second, how many jobs are crap. But we were putting a very middle-class frame on the research, assuming everyone wants to progress. What many people want is a few extra quid, and to be able to go home at the right time for the kids. For many people, the most important thing is *autonomy* — having control over your life.'

Settling for a job with reasonably clear boundaries, a strict wage-labour contract with no expectation of development or progression on the one side and no claim on the employee's time beyond what is paid for on the other: it's a realpolitik aspect of choice.

Choosing time

Another decision to be made is how much to work. Part-time women, we know, lose out on pay and careers. How far do they choose this way of working?

In a recent MumsNet survey, 70% of part-time working women with young children felt that they had freely chosen to work part-time. Almost all worked full-time before having children, and two-thirds planned to increase their working hours once their children were older. 'For many, their decision to work part-time reflects their preference for being more involved in bringing up their children than they could be if working full-time,' the report noted. 'Many said that they did not want to miss out on the important early years in their child's life.'[18]

MumsNet respondents may not be typical, and we don't know what trade-offs they are making and how painful these are. Ideally, of course, we would like to know whether they will say the same in 10 or 15 years, when maybe the impact or otherwise of that choice in terms of career advancement will be apparent. But, for now, they don't appear to be in much doubt that they've made a choice.

The context of the debate is changing. It's not only that the numbers of part-timers have increased significantly as a consequence of the current economic crisis. A far higher proportion of those working part-time now say that they would prefer to work longer hours. But the discussion is largely stuck in an increasingly absurd and damaging polarisation between full-timers and part-timers, as if these are two discrete and homogeneous categories. This, patently, is not the case. 'Part-time', which the Office of National Statistics defines as working 30 hours a week or fewer, covers a very broad range of commitments, from working just a couple of hours to making a time commitment as great as or greater than many 'full-timers'. Many people's official hours in one job are just a little under the threshold that divides full-time from part-time, but they often work over that limit; bracketing them with someone who puts in a couple of mornings a week is unhelpful, to say the least. Others work several part-time jobs, each of which might be quite small but which add up to a total of hours that, in a single job, would be classified as full-time or more (leaving aside all the time they spend getting from one job to another). This is an essential plank in the argument we shall come on to in the final chapter for a different approach to income, taxation, and benefits.

Vertical careers: not always the best choice?

Choosing a lateral career

We met Tim in Chapter 5, talking with his partner, Freda, about ambition. He has made his way in theatre, to which he has been committed since the age of 12. He has stayed with this, getting experience in a range of roles and making a positive choice about what he wanted to work at within his chosen occupation. But this is very different from looking onwards and upwards. He has not intentionally given himself a wider set of opportunities. Yet he has moved from going up and down ladders as an electrician to overseeing the theatre's technical operations, which puts him above stage manager in the theatre hierarchy (my observation, not his). Tim illustrates that it is possible to have a career where you are committed, and work hard at it, but are not ambitious, and do it because you think it is worthwhile rather than because it will take you anywhere further.

Wilma, whom we have also met before, is 34 and the deputy general secretary of a small trade union. Her story encapsulates many of the issues raised above. She referred early on in our discussion to having a young daughter, whose care her partner shares. It emerged later that she has two other children, sons by her first marriage, now aged 18 and 16. So Wilma was an early parent, and her school achievements suffered. Exactly as Denny did in *Educating Rita*, her first husband expected her to go on having children and stay at home to look after them, but this was not how she saw things.

Since taking a different route, Wilma has always made a priority of education as a route to career advancement. Studying and gaining qualifications (in her case, in both the formal education system and the union movement) have been almost an article of faith for her, and she feels even more strongly that it is something which women generally should be encouraged to pursue. Wilma is justifiably proud of the progress she has made to her current position. Now, however, she faces something of a dilemma. Her path upwards is blocked, mainly because of the structure of the union that employs her. She has spent eight years in her current job. Her egalitarian domestic arrangements mean that she can spend more time with her daughter than she managed with her sons, and she feels comfortable in her position in 'the food chain of the workplace', the vivid metaphor she used to describe the position of a male colleague earlier on in this chapter. But she blushed when she said this, and acknowledged her discomfort at feeling comfortable, because it seemed to her to be inconsistent with her persistent striving for improvement. She felt that in some sense she was betraying her credo of a working woman's duty to advance. 'I've taken my foot off the pedal, which is very, very naughty of me. I'm getting more involved in other things. Don't get me wrong, I'm still going to do my stuff, but now I'm just okay. It's highly embarrassing to admit.'

But she then told me that she had become a magistrate two years previously and was already sitting on a specialist panel on domestic violence. She is also updating one of her work qualifications. This is hardly what most of us would consider coasting, for a parent with three children. But having driven herself to break out of the original and unwelcome pathway identified for her, and preaching to her union members the virtues of education as a route upwards and the need for women to take advantage of career opportunities, she had these values so deeply entrenched that she felt visible discomfort at the idea that she had deviated from them.

Wilma's is a fine example of a lateral career pattern, mixing paid and unpaid work with professional development but outside the framework of a vertical ladder. She is coming to terms with this turn. 'I'll concede the choice thing. I've made choices. If you move sideways, you can get a lot of satisfaction.'

So civic activity can provide an outlet for competences where standard careers don't offer themselves. Betty's original desire, after leaving grammar school, was to go into gardening. She went off to horticultural college and got a qualification, but she couldn't get a job as a gardener. So she has worked in local government, in various jobs, gaining substantial experience. Meanwhile, she has done various courses, including at Open University, but neither the experience nor the qualifications have enabled her to progress: 'The skills I've picked up don't fit into the structure ... I would have had to go back with a job at Scale 5 or 6, more likely 5, with a manager over me and no responsibilities. So in that respect everything I've done over the last 20 years would not be recognised.'

She now does not think there is a future for her in her paid work, and is turning to use her skills in local politics.

Lauren's story also shows how choice can be more than an individual act, and how it can be made horizontally. Both she and her husband had established themselves in promising initial careers, he as a social worker and she in teaching. They wanted to leave London, and agreed that they would go wherever the first opening came up. It turned out to be in her husband's field, but Lauren has not resented this. She found, or rather created, a job at the local school, where she set up a department providing language education for overseas students and training mainstream teachers with bilingual pupils in their classes. This was highly rewarding. After a while, she was asked informally whether she would consider going up the ladder, beyond being a departmental head, but decided not to do that. She preferred 'horizontal achievement' — continuing to develop her department, to do voluntary work, and to have a good work–life balance. (Lauren also described her local beauty salon. It has a nearly all-woman staff with a male manager; so far, so typical. But he manages it in a very non-hierarchical way, and in addition arranges it so that the staff can rotate around different functions, and so deploy their full range of skills if they wish. She describes it as a very happy place.)

The word 'career' has a misleadingly planned and purposive flavour (slightly paradoxically, since 'careering' means a lack of control). Many of the jobs that women hold do not form into a coherent sequence that would find a place in the handbook of a sober careers adviser. Their employment records twist and turn, with dips and gaps. They may not have 'chosen' all of the steps in the sequence, and are even less likely to have chosen the actual sequence itself. (As ever, this applies also to men, but not to the same degree.) This does not mean these steps do not make sense.

For me, there is an important distinction between these two types of 'career': one that goes sideways, or even downwards, when measured against the conventional dimensions of pay and status, but that is the result of choice, or at least deliberate risk-taking; and one that takes a trajectory that is twisted by external constraints against the wishes of the individual concerned. Yet it is not an easy distinction to draw. As Kierkegaard famously said: 'Life can only be understood backwards, but has to be lived forwards.' The same might be said of many careers. What is clear, however, is that we would all be better off if we could operate in a context where lateral and diagonal moves, and interrupted trajectories, are not just tolerated but also recognised as legitimate components of careers, for men as well as women. To quote another philosopher, this time Kant: 'Out of the crooked timber of humanity no straight thing was ever made.' Maybe there are fewer and fewer 'straight-line' careers, and the lesson is that we should work with the grain of the work–time timber, not against it.

The Peter Principle and a horizontal career: John's story

John was a miner in the Llynfi valley in South Wales who told me his story at a conference on adult learning. After ten years of working with machinery, he became a fitter, 'a spanner being lighter than a shovel'. Then he hit what he called a glass ceiling — an unusual application of the image, given first that he's a man and secondly that he was working underground …

He applied for a job teaching first aid, at a mining training centre above ground. He worked at the training centre for ten years, but suffered from a crisis of confidence — who was he to be a teacher in a white coat, without a qualification to his name? He suffered, in other words, from the imposter syndrome (see Chapter 6).

Fortunately, the crisis led to positive outcomes. John got himself a personal tutor in basic skills. After two years, the tutor sent him on to do O levels, first in English and maths, and then in physics. This led on to enrolment in Open University, to undertake a degree in humanities. While waiting for the Open University course to start, he did a course in computers. He gained several promotions, going from a basic mining instructor to an advanced mining instructor to introducing computers into colliery training offices and training the staff, and eventually to colliery training manager, responsible for the teaching of 1,100 staff.

Not all went well — John was made redundant, and got a job in a supermarket, which he hated, since the boss was always telling him what to do whereas he was used to being trusted to do his job. So he left that, went on to a teacher training course, and now devotes himself to and teaches his hobby: embroidery.

John's story is a partial example of the Peter Principle — promotion above his level of competence. But it was he who saw his own incompetence and decided to do something about it. He made a positive choice that opened up further opportunities: onward progression both educationally and professionally. A miner with a horizontal career — a forerunner of the future?

I started this chapter by voicing reservations about choice as an unalloyed good. Yet making good choices — ones that are appropriate to individual circumstances and values — is something that surely concerns almost all of us. A major driver in many people's choice of occupation and career remains the material one of earning money. As a generalisation, this applies more strongly to men than women. But as women's earnings become a more significant part of many households,[19] the onus on men to earn should, in principle, be reduced. So the case for more careers with more diverse shapes — crooked timber structures rather than straight ones of concrete and glass — applies perhaps even more to men. How we can achieve such reverse convergence, as I call it, is the subject of the next chapter.

9

The Paula Agenda

What is to be done?

Half of the story in the previous chapters has been about the extraordinary expansion of women's opportunities. Think back to George Eliot's Maggie Tulliver and Winifred Holtby's Lydia Holly, and what was open, or rather not open, to them. Virginia Woolf's *Three Guineas* is another biting indictment of the grossly unequal support given to men's and women's learning: Arthur's education fund supports him generously through the noble quadrangles of Oxford and Cambridge, but his sister has to make do with classes given by 'a little woman with a red nose who is not well educated herself but has an invalid mother to support'.[1] If Woolf and her fellow authors could have peered ahead to the educational crossovers recounted in Chapter 2, they would have found them literally fantastic.

These educational achievements have undoubtedly had their effect. Women are expected to aspire occupationally. Young women with good qualifications today start professional careers on more or less equal terms with their male peers. The overall pay gap has narrowed, so that women earn closer to male rates. In politics, there has been a dramatic upsurge in women leaders: in my own patch, we have a female prime minister of the United Kingdom, and the three main parties in Scotland are each led by a woman; for a time the

United States of America looked set to elect its first woman president. But big questions remain about the direction and pace of future progress. Will the hard-won initial parity in careers be sustained over time, as women and men follow different trajectories? Can women in lower-ranking jobs benefit as much as their higher-flying sisters do? Can the way we as societies reward people be adapted to reflect the different values and styles that women bring to the workplace?

The Paula Principle matters. It matters to very many individual women because they cannot put to full use the competences they have acquired, in youth and in adulthood. This means personal frustration as well as material loss, feeling undervalued as much as being underpaid. It matters to organisations (profit or non-profit) that are missing out on the skills available to them. It matters to societies, if they genuinely subscribe to the simple basic principles of fairness and efficiency. The costs — personal, economic, and social — are rising all the time as women continue to accumulate qualifications and skills, and at a faster rate than men do.

It would be a big step forward if we could agree that the issues raised by the Paula Principle affect us all, men as well as women. Even then, not everyone will see these issues in the same light. Opinions will differ, sometimes sharply, on which aspects matter most. That's why I've invited you to reflect on which of the PP factors you think are particularly important, for yourself or more generally. Does the first PP factor, discrimination, still have as much of a grip as it used to? Is it easier now to reconcile childcare with paid work, and are we heading for the same struggle with eldercare (PP factor two)? Has women's self-confidence grown along with their qualifications, or do we need to change the ways we reward 'confidence' (PP factor three)? And are we near to dissolving the circular process by which social and professional networks favour men's careers at the expense of those of women (PP factor four)?

The final factor takes us in an apparently contrary direction. Some women choose not to climb further up a career ladder, but instead to continue doing what they are competently doing. Or they choose to move sideways — or even drop down a level or two — because this offers a more fulfilling future. These positive choices made by some women provide us not with a reason for complacency about the current position but with a potential template for *both* sexes in their pursuit of a better quality of working and personal life.

How do we take this forward? In other words, what is the Paula Agenda?

Changing career models: from the ladder to the mosaic

In *The Mismeasure of Women*, social psychologist Carol Tavris discusses the 'normalcy' of man, the notion that things are measured by reference to the male sex.[2] This, she argues, has generated three perspectives: a) that men are normal, and women different and deficient; b) that men are normal, and women opposite and superior; and c) that men are normal, and women should be more like them — what you might call the Henry Higgins position.[3] The common element in all cases is, evidently, that the male pattern is the norm. Her case is that we should think, instead, of reshaping the norm itself. This applies exactly to the implications of the Paula Principle.

The basic challenge is this: how to topple the dominant model, which holds that the only pattern that really counts as a meaningful career is full-time employment, sustained more or less continuously over a working life, with vertical progression. Fewer and fewer working lives actually conform to this model, as a career pattern or as a symbol of work commitment. And yet it is still this — the ladder model — that sits in the heads of most of our policy-makers, employers, trade unionists, and, probably, our colleagues too. It's the perceived norm, from which any deviation is highly risky.

What alternatives are there to the ladder? A mosaic might just fit the bill. Mosaics may be regular or irregular. They can include components of very varying sizes, shapes, and colours. So a mosaic career might include a mix of full-time and other employment; working part-time for long or short periods; taking a break or breaks from paid work; changing occupations; or moving sideways or even downwards. A mosaic career may be planned, as when someone takes a break to look after children, or exploratory, as when they realise that they need to try out new pathways. The pattern may emerge only in retrospect, but someone operating on this basis is just as likely to be committed to their work as a single-minded careerist. They may not have the in-depth expertise of the traditional ladder-climber, but they may well bring other, broader, experience and skills. Either way, their skills deserve recognition.

This change in attitudes is unlikely if the issue is seen primarily as one for women. So the next proposition is that the revaluing will only happen if more men let go of the full-time continuous work model. This is basic realpolitik: the more men follow mosaic careers, the more women will be able to exercise their competences and be duly rewarded for them. This is the most likely route by which those work patterns that are currently seen as non-standard can gain proper acceptance.

If the arguments are all phrased around what women need in order to pursue successful mosaic careers, the changes will probably occur, eventually. But it will be a far longer and more uneven process than if we concentrate on how men can be enabled to loosen the full-time straitjacket. So, although some of the Paula Agenda outlined below is a restatement of familiar items such as better childcare provision and supportive mentoring for women, the central thrust of it is different: it is to enable more men to ditch the assumption that full-time continuous work is the only way to pursue a career.

It is, indubitably, harder for men to make this shift. Lesley, the policy adviser and former Gingerbread staffer, made the point: 'I've got a male friend working at the BBC. He went on to a four-day week in his early 30s, after having the first of his two children. His friends queried it, saying' — here her voice rose — '"What are you doing?" as though he was no long serious about his career — even though they are all, to a man, North London liberal intelligentsia. You don't get much of a more positive environment in which to make that choice. But people were horrified, which I found very weird.'

If a youngish man in that kind of milieu can't reduce his work time by just 20% without being seen as giving up on his career, it gives us some indication of just how deep-rooted in the male psyche is full-time continuous work.

Reverse convergence

The United Kingdom is, despite some dispute on the statistics, the long-hours champion of Europe — at least for men.[4] This hits them at both ends of the earnings spectrum: poor men work long hours of overtime to make up some kind of halfway decent wage, while, in return for their bigger package, rich men consign themselves to the corporation, body and perhaps soul. British women do not work longer than their European sisters, but are affected too: as full-time workers, they hit the same barriers as men — except they hit them harder if they work in organisations where long hours are part of the culture, with evening and weekend events gobbling up free or family time. And, as 'part-time' workers, they may forsake careers that come in wrappers marked 'full-time only'. Many poorer women have to put together several jobs to make a living, piecing out their work and care time. Redesigning this temporal mosaic — in its daily, weekly, annual, and lifelong forms — is the single most important step to getting rid of the negative aspects of the Paula Principle.

Harvard economist Claudia Goldin used her 2014 presidential address to the American Economic Association to tackle what she called the 'last chapter' in the 'grand convergence'.[5] By this she meant that women had moved into paid employment in increasing numbers, often worked full-time, studied across a wider range of subjects than they used to, and had careers across a wider range of occupations. Yet, as she points out, the pay gap had not disappeared. Why not? Goldin is adamant. When you take all factors into account, she says, it is not because women are segregated into different occupations, or any of the other standard explanations; it is because of *the different rewards paid to those who depart from the conventional full-time continuous employment pattern*. So, she argues, the pay gap will close only if we pay attention to time regimes at work — the hours worked, the schedules, and the degree of flexibility — and make sure these fit with the competences of those in the occupation.

Goldin backs up her case with an array of sophisticated statistics. As you can guess, I buy it. But I take issue with her notion that this would be the last chapter in a 'grand convergence'. As we know, the convergence has overwhelmingly been by women towards male patterns of behaviour and attitudes. How much *reciprocal* movement has there been? We can easily underestimate how much change has occurred in men's general attitudes and behaviour towards women at work but, when it comes to their own working time, the full-time continuous model is still pretty firmly in place. As political writer Gaby Hinsliff put it in her excellently reasoned *Half a Wife*: 'We are not going to get anywhere until we understand exactly why the standard 40-46-40 model — working 40 hours a week, for 46 weeks a year, for the next 40 years of your life — has such a powerful hold on employers' imagination.'[6]

It's not only the employers' imagination that is gripped. In August 2014, *The Guardian* reported that the numbers of men working part-time had increased by 47,000 to over two million in the last year, compared with more than six million women. The piece highlighted the case of the chief economist of Lloyds Banking Group, Patrick

Foley, who had shifted to a three-day week in order to write books, run triathlons — and pursue non-executive directorships. It's an encouraging example in its way. But Patrick is hardly representative of the average earner, and at least one of his pursuits will presumably make up for his loss of regular earnings — if indeed he needs to do that. The other case highlighted in the article is more typical: Luke Sudbery, a systems engineer in a London university, is also going onto a three-day week after the birth of his daughter. He had no difficulty in persuading his employer to agree. But it hasn't been plain sailing: 'There is sometimes the impression that I'm skiving. Nothing is said explicitly, it's just jokes. I do have to remind people I'm not actually getting paid for my days off.' It matters where you are in the hierarchy.

The article goes on to quote Karen Mattison, joint chief executive of Timewise, a pioneering agency set up to match women and men to well-paying part-time jobs: '[For] men who have gone part-time at a later stage in their career, in a sense there is an acceptance that it is a lifestyle choice. People in their 30s and 40s may be more nervous about being openly part-time. We've seen, in our own research, that they are worried they will be passed over for promotion.'[7] So our theatre manager Tim (see Chapter 5) is still very much an exception in his easy acceptance of the consequences of going part-time. Most of the males doing part-time jobs are doing so against their wishes, as they currently express them. They say they would rather be working the full whack. The usual reason given is that they need the money; this is hard to argue against, but I wonder how much it is also because they feel that anything else is not a 'proper' job. 'Real men don't work part-time' is how one production worker expressed it in an Australian study.[8]

Claudia Goldin's 'convergence' suggests that the expected — and desired — outcome is some kind of fusion into a single line, with no eventual difference between men and women in their earnings or careers. Historically, and still in many respects today, this has been the primary aim of many of those concerned with equality, understandably so. But as far as the Paula Principle is concerned, this focuses our attention on the wrong thing. You could say that it's not ambitious enough. As we have seen, women now bring more human capital to the party than men do, so if they were fully and directly rewarded for this, there should be not convergence but crossover, in pay as well as competence. Equality in this sense would mean equal rewards for similar levels of qualification — and therefore actually put women ahead. But we should also ask this question: do male careers provide such a good norm that convergence on them is the ideal goal? The political sociologist Gøsta Esping-Andersen argues that the masculinisation of the female life course may have gone as far as it reasonably can, and we should be thinking more about the possible feminisation of the male life course.[9] I agree. Kant, we saw, talked of the crooked timber of humanity: instead of crooked females behaving like straight males, more straight males should take on the shape of crooked females (I speak, of course, only of their working lives). It's time for more men's career patterns to bend to the feminine norm.

There's a dual motion here. Women will go on moving into conventional male patterns of work but, at the same time, more men will, at some point or points in their working lives, start to adopt patterns traditionally associated with women. Mainly this means not working full-time but building in career breaks, parental leaves, sabbaticals, reduced annual hours, and so on, all the way through to stepped retirement.[10] These are all ways of breaking up the full-time continuous model into smaller and less uniform pieces. Building up mosaic careers means changes in our personal attitudes; in the way employers and managers organise things; and in the way our tax and benefit 'systems' operate. It's a shift that involves many different levels.

The reverse-convergence image gets us away from the idea that there is a single, ideal, gender-free way of organising careers. More men than women are still likely to work full-time, for more of their lives. More women than men are still likely to choose to spend much time looking after small children. Exact symmetry is not the ideal, but that does not mean that the current patterns on either of these dimensions are satisfactory. Reverse convergence would mean that the spread of realistic options is broader and stronger, for both sexes. Paula can construct her mosaic career without feeling that she is betraying her values, while Peter can do the same without feeling that he is deviating too dangerously from the norm.

Much of the difference between the Peter and the Paula Principles boils down to what is seen as 'normal'. For Peter, the working 'career' is defined very much as a continuous rising through the ranks — and the challenge is to prevent so many incompetent people from rising as high as they currently do. Paula shares in large measure the meritocratic rationale: more women should be able to put their competences to better use, and be rewarded for them. But this cannot happen within a framework that clings so tenaciously to the traditional norm of a full-time and, as far as possible, uninterrupted working life.

Symmetry between women and men in this respect is a false as well as doomed aspiration. The norm itself — a male one — is out of time.[11]

Women are infinitely more likely than men to face choices about changing career status — moving out of employment, or into some form of part-time employment, and then trying to move back into a job at roughly the same level as before.[12] Such decisions follow one another in a cumulative process over Paula's life course, with major consequences for pay, status, and satisfaction. Women are better educated than they used to be, have higher expectations for themselves and their lives, and they know they will live longer. This is a powerful combination. Yet employers have demonstrably not caught up with this combination of demographic and social change. In 1984, just 13% of older women thought employers gave them too few opportunities; now that figure is 70%.[13] Surely the solution can only be a richer and more diverse pattern of working time, across the longer lifespan.

The future of work: direction unknown?

The Paula Agenda

So this brings to the Paula Agenda. I move quickly through the first five items on the agenda, not because they are unimportant but because they have been discussed by others in greater depth and with far more authority. I discuss item six in more detail.

1. Reduce inequalities

This is more of a broad background challenge than an agenda item, but it is too important to omit. Gross inequality has a particular relevance to the Paula Principle because it deforms the reward system so grotesquely. Women come off worse in conditions of high inequality, and have less chance of seeing their talents recognised.

The stratospheric pay packages of the top 1% hardly ever accrue to women, but they affect the lives of women very strongly.

There is a mounting consensus, across different political positions, on the need to contain the vast differences in what people get for doing a day's work.[14] Capping bankers' bonuses may be popular, but is a marginal and probably ineffectual move; those targeted will simply pay for agile legal brains to circumvent lawmakers' intentions. I am much more encouraged by the emerging drive for a stronger overall moral climate of fairness in business. Shareholders and citizens together can — and increasingly do — reject grossly excessive demands, and challenge the practices and systems that support them, on the grounds that they are not right, ethically or commercially. This gets us closer to asking why particular jobs are valued and rewarded as they are, and to putting responsibility where it belongs, instead of dumping it in the lap of abstract and often manipulated 'market forces'.

Building a hard-nosed case for greater equality, one that combines moral and economic aspects, is definitely on the cards.[15] A recent recruit to the cause is the OECD, not known as a soft touch on economic issues.[16] A normative limit on the ratio between top and average/lowest earners is attainable; grotesquely inflated payments that have no business rationale are not too hard to spot.[17] More generally, we need reward systems in organisations of all kinds that more accurately and fairly reflect merit (see page 202, item 5). When social activist and Labour politician Michael Young coined the term meritocracy back in 1958, it was to describe a dystopia, a rather heartless society where those without 'merit' would be discarded. Meritocracy now has a less negative aura, and the Paula Principle assumes that merit should indeed be rewarded. But meritocracies can only work if the measures of merit are fair and if they do not lead to unacceptable inequality.

2. Prioritise universal and affordable childcare, and meet the eldercare challenge

Better childcare is essential, for everyone's sake: children, parents, and society. The Paula Principle reflects how the current inadequacies of provision for childcare impose a massive tax on (mainly) women's income, which lasts a lifetime. The logic of Brenda's comment on page 103, when she recommends her mentees to look on childcare as an investment, applies to society as much as to the individual. It is at the collective level that childcare can be much more effectively and fairly implemented. We could do with more rigorous but broad calculations of the economic and social impact of better childcare, accepting that the results will pay out — to us all — over a timespan of at least three decades.

PP factor two, issues connected with caring responsibilities, attracted more votes than any other from visitors to the website as an explanation for the Paula Principle. The evidence is very clear that having children is often the key point at which women's careers tail off. The brevity of the discussion of it here as an agenda item in no way reflects its salience to the Paula Principle. I simply have nothing original to say in support of better, cheaper, and more accessible childcare beyond what has already been said by others at great and valuable length.[18]

At the other end of the life course, we need to anticipate the enormous growth in the need for services for older people. Momentum is building behind the right to take time off work for caring for older people. The traditional patching of professional services (public and private), on the one hand, and informal care, on the other, will not suffice. Innovations such as the Circle Movement represent a viable way forward. Circle is a membership organisation for older people that offers social and practical support to all of its members. Members participate in a variety of monthly events, where they connect with people who share their interests. They can reach out for practical help in and around the home, delivered by trustworthy local helpers.[19]

Such initiatives need amplification and support. Otherwise, we will see more and more older women increasingly qualified but dropping out of the labour force, dampening or dousing their later career aspirations in order to care for the previous generation. This will mean a huge loss of skill and experience. As with childcare, we could do with sensible analyses of the benefits and costs of good eldercare, and a much broader discussion of the implications of our ageing societies.

3. Expand guidance services and mentoring networks

Melissa Benn's *What Should We Tell Our Daughters?* explores how to advise young women on dealing with the contradictory pressures that modern life throws up for them. She argues very strongly that girls (and boys) need a fuller chance to explore what type of work might suit them. So do women (and men). We need broader and better guidance on careers, and then effective mentoring and support systems.[20]

'Careers guidance' maybe brings to mind a specific and rather narrowly defined service (one that is currently very much under attack in the United Kingdom), whereas what is needed is a range of different sources of advice, information, and experience. I'd emphasise the experience angle. Giving young people direct access to different occupations so that they can actually see, smell, and feel them is surely more likely to be effective than merely imparting information, however well designed.[21] That kind of work experience should be an integral element of the curriculum, to a far greater extent than it currently is. The challenge is to make sure that Paula has access to the same range of experience as Peter — and vice-versa.

However successfully this is done at school, it will not be enough. For many years, the mantra has been that we'll all have to change occupations many times in our working lives. It is certainly the case that people both want and have to change as they get older, if they are to flourish. Careers guidance should be available throughout people's careers; it is a yawning gap in our services.[22] We need a mindshift: the mosaic career, with its variety of timing and changes of direction, means that guidance should be routinely available over the working life. Mosaic careers need regular opportunities to work out how to fit the pieces together.

Mentoring addresses PP factor four, the absence of vertical networks. Schemes such as the Million Women Mentors are wonderful examples of such network building.[23] They boost women's opportunities to link to people at higher levels, not just to their peers. There are role models for all women (and men) who might buck the trend — by going into 'minority' occupations or aspiring to reach positions that they would otherwise never have considered. The role models do not have to be high-flying superstars, just the kinds of people who would encourage others to emulate them. The internet makes it a whole lot easier than it used to be to muster and disseminate sources of information to enable women to envisage themselves moving up and along.[24]

4. Enable learning throughout life

We need to take a radical look at formal and informal learning across the life course, and how it can be better supported. We've seen how women such as Iona, Mandy, and Vanessa had the chance, through UnionLearn, to give themselves a whole new identity, beyond anything they had dreamt about as young women. The case for rebalancing our education systems so that they offer opportunities at every age and stage, and not only in youth, has never been stronger. Our longer lives give the case for lifelong learning a further powerful shove.[25]

Women will always have to cope with more twists and turns in their lives than men, and most of these will generate some kind of learning challenge. So for them there is an inherent lifelong driver of educational need. Chapter 2 showed how women take greater advantage of adult-learning opportunities, personal and professional. One important step forward would be a better system for recognising the competences that they acquire, formally and informally. Some countries are well ahead in their recognition of prior and experiential learning.

The options for mixing different kinds of learning — face-to-face, online and off — have never been more diverse and potentially rich. But in the United Kingdom, the current set of opportunities is under severe threat: adult community classes are disappearing; part-time courses at all levels are being cut; and, because the public sector is shrinking, its training provision, which favours women, is melting away.

A flourishing culture of lifelong learning goes hand in hand with greater gender equality and a respect for individual choices. Populations that engage in learning are more likely to treat one another as equal citizens. It is no coincidence that adults in Scandinavian countries are such keen participants in adult education, with something like two in every three participating every year in some form or other. Dark winter evenings may have something to do with it, but adult learning and equality for all citizens are two cultural facets that are closely interlinked.[26]

Enabling lifelong learning is a recommendation that applies with equal — no, greater — force to men. If, as I have argued, undermining the Paula Principle means men breaking their bondage to full-time continuous working, they need good access to learning opportunities of different kinds. We have seen how men participate significantly less than women in almost every form of adult education. Breaking the traditional work-time model would help with this, but we could do with more imaginative thinking about how to motivate or inspire them to see themselves as lifelong learners. The 'men's sheds' movement, originating in Australia, is one good example.[27] So let's leave the lip service behind, and make the commitment to lifelong learning a genuine one. A system of individual learning accounts, built up and drawn upon over each citizen's life, would be a fine start.[28]

5. Design reward systems to more accurately reflect real value

The market principle is usually the least bad way of determining how people should be rewarded for working. Markets can often account for preferences and needs, skills and effort, better than dictators, monopolies, committees, or lotteries. But everyone, barring a few fundamentalists, recognises that even quite sophisticated forms of markets do not always work. In a sense, indeed, the Paula Principle is all about a large-scale market failure: it is clear that women are not being rewarded 'correctly' for their competences.

We know that there is a significant difference between men and women in how they perceive rewards, and how these are related to their own judgements of their value.[29] Men, on the whole, will see their pay as the index of what they are worth, and so if they can push up their pay they are not only getting more money but also raising their sense of self-worth. For them, the relationship between pay and value is very close. Women are more likely to have a broader sense of their value, which takes into account what the market pays but also includes an intrinsic sense of the value of what they do. This certainly has its advantages: it endows women with more of what American sociologist David Riesman famously called 'inner direction'.[30] But the crunch comes when the gap between value and reward is stretched too far, and when women find out that others are treated differently (as Nuala expressed so vividly on page 80).

The central question is how well our reward systems reflect what they are supposed to reflect: skill, effort, commitment, and achievement. It's not an easy thing to manage, but some organisations do very much better than others. Where rewards are poorly aligned to competence, this is in part about weakness and exploitation, especially in low-paid occupations. Managers, consciously or (probably more often) unconsciously, find it easier to offer women career ladders that have fewer steps upwards and a longer time gap between the rungs.

At the other end of the spectrum, executive bonuses are often determined by how far the employee is prepared to negotiate, to be noisy about their own performance, and generally rattle the cage. Some conclude that women should behave similarly in order to gain equal treatment. What does this say about the quality of the organisation's judgements on the actual worth of what someone does? Is table-banging a valuable skill? The logic is hard to accept. As Anne-Marie Slaughter, who has reached the top in both academic and political employment, said: 'If women are ever to achieve real equality as leaders, then we have to stop accepting male behaviour and male choices as the default and the ideal.'[31]

It is easy enough to agree that we need systems that reflect actual skills, but there is no royal route to this. Brenda's example of the language of skills (Chapter 7) is very telling: women's language, she said, 'is about "we", about looking for *complementary skills* in a team, recognising that they themselves cannot do it all. For men, it is about "I"; competitive; their personal career.' Women give weight to a collective as much as to an individual set of skills. 'Teamwork' is a competence for which employers very commonly say that they look, but how well does this get assessed and rewarded in practice?

This is a broad cultural issue as much as one looking for technical managerial answers. We need to start by taking a fresh look at how our organisations' reward systems work, thinking specifically of how they might take better account of those competences that are more often found in women. But it is also a matter of what kinds of respect we give to different kinds of behaviour and attitudes in our own daily lives.

6. Take a new approach to working time

If we are to dethrone the full-time continuous working model, and support the idea of a mosaic working life, the time is right for a fresh approach to how we put jobs into temporal categories. What do 'part-time', 'flexible hours', or 'non-scheduled work' actually mean: variable hours per day, days per week, hours per year, or what exactly? Such questions are part of a broader debate on the positive effects of reducing working time.

At various points in history, people have made the case for radically shortening the amount of time we spend at work. The arguments have come from quite different political standpoints: famously from the economist John Maynard Keynes, who predicted that we would get down to a 15-hour week as a simple consequence of economic progress, and more recently from the New Economics Foundation, with their case for a 21-hour week, and from technology analysts who fear the impact of a massive spread of automation.[32] I'm not going to rerun these arguments but will frame them in a life-course perspective, in order to give even more power to their various elbows.

Keynes and others understandably focus mainly on the smaller units of time — the day, the week, or even the year. But this obscures the trajectories of people's working lives, and the inevitable extension of these working lives in coming decades. We've seen that it is trajectories that count: the paths traced by women's employment over time, relative to that of men. My simple argument is that the stretching of working life offers a real opportunity for reconciling some of the fundamental tensions exposed by the Paula Principle.

Of course, we could be as wrong about the inevitability of longer working lives as Keynes was about shorter working weeks. But if not, and if we can subvert the psychological dominance of the full-time model, then space opens up for a major renegotiation of work time. This would remove at least some of the pressure on women and men with any kind of aspiration to keep clambering upwards on the job ladder, without interruption and as fast as they can. It would mean that people will have a different *temporal framework* within which to make their career, and the definition of 'career' will be more variable. More occupations will be open to late entrants, and to re-entrants. It will be easier to switch to a different trade or professional identity; to move sideways or even downwards without this being seen as a failure; and to step out and step back in to work. The spread of such mosaic patterns will potentially benefit both men and women enormously.

Not everyone is keen to work longer, of course. Some are tired of work, or just tired, and cannot wait to stop. Ill health is a significant factor, especially for those who have had to work for much of their lives in harsh conditions. But to some extent, working later is simply inevitable if we in Western societies are to sustain anything like even the kind of pension support we have now — patchy though that often is.[33] As importantly, many people do actively want to carry on working beyond what are still regarded as retirement ages, for social as well as financial reasons. Even more would choose to if the circumstances were right: the crucial consideration is whether they can do so in a pattern that suits them.

What options would this involve? We could work a shorter day and avoid daily commuter crush; work a shorter week and enjoy longer weekends, with proper time for grandchildren or leisure pursuits; work only part of the year and have a real stretch of recuperation or exploration time. At the risk of sounding like a promotional blurb for Saga (which sells insurance and holidays to over-55s), these are indeed the factors that change people's attitudes towards work. Only some kinds of work truly require permanent presence in the office or factory.[34] For Paula, the clincher is that a longer working life with a pattern of flexible and part-time work will prise loose the grip of the traditional full-time model across the life course as a whole. Working 'part-time' will no longer be the deviant or subservient pattern, but the norm.

What might bring this about?

a. Limit the 'part-time' label to eight hours or less

Our current dividing line between 'full-time' and 'part-time' work (a line that varies from 30 hours in the United Kingdom to 35 in the United States, and 37.5 in Australia) is truly bizarre. There is no way of drawing a line that is not to some extent arbitrary, but this one is way out. Some people argue for abolishing the notion of part-time altogether, but it would only creep in through the back door. So I suggest flipping the focus around and drawing the line at eight hours — roughly the length of one working day. If you work fewer hours than this per week, then work is probably a minor part of your life (notwithstanding the experience of fictional gardening columnist Daisy Flett in Chapter 3).

Changing statistical categories is a major operation. Quite understandably, the authorities are reluctant to do this, partly through bureaucratic inertia but also because it messes up trends: you can't compare data from previous years with data gathered using new categories. But categories are supposed to simplify things, not distort them: when a category is an active block on progress, it needs to go. Drawing the chief dividing line at 30, 35, or 37.5 hours is a prime example of looking at things from the male end of the telescope. Switching to eight hours is a meaningful division, as it is more or less equivalent to a conventional working day, and it has the added virtue of highlighting the importance of 'smaller' jobs. The 30-, 35-, or 37.5-hour category could be maintained in some form to allow continuity of data collection, but the eight-hour limit would provide the principal defining line.

b. Give flexibility legal impetus

The default position should be that all jobs are available on a flexible basis, unless there is a good business reason for this not to be the case. When the Foresight Project on Mental Capital, sponsored by the UK's Chief Scientist, tackled the measures needed to improve mental and physical wellbeing, it backed up the case for flexible working with analysis that suggests substantial economic as well as social gains.[35] We in the United Kingdom already have the right to request flexible work, but this needs strengthening. The principle of *flexibility as default* should extend to the way jobs are advertised, and more generally to the way career paths are presented. There are lessons to be drawn from the experience of countries such as the Netherlands, where legislation enforces strong rights for part-timers to enjoy equal career opportunities (see Chapter 4).

The UK Parliamentary Select Committee on Women and Equality has pointed the way forward: 'Our key recommendation is that all jobs should be available to work flexibly unless an employer can demonstrate an immediate and continuing business case against doing so.'[36] There is only so much that legislation can do. Change will happen much faster if managers get on board, resulting in cultural adjustments within organisations. The public sector already plays a front-runner role here, but is flanked by other organisations that also see the commercial case for retaining as well as attracting talent in this way. Finally, change needs to extend to all levels of the organisation, and not just to high fliers.

c. Make full use of new technologies

Our capacity to link up in all kinds of novel and immediate ways makes diverse working patterns a realistic possibility and not a pipe dream. Communication technologies beget networks that have both flexibility and reliability. In the United Kingdom, initiatives such as Timewise (whose joint CEO Emma Stewart I interviewed) do a great job finding opportunities for women who want to work in high-quality part-time jobs. Slivers of Time is another organisation that starts from the position that people want to do paid or unpaid work in a whole variety of time patterns, and uses new technology to meet those needs.[37]

A particular value of both models is that they can be put into practice in different forms, to suit local needs. Of course, there is no smooth and wholly harmonious way of matching people and opportunities, but a localised network can operate with higher levels of trust and flexibility and stands a better chance of success.

More broadly, we have the opportunity to create new markets in time. If this sounds like a neoliberal fantasy, think again. Too many people, especially women, are shut out from work because they cannot find jobs with a time schedule they can manage. Connecting them to employers who can offer work that suits their schedule has become much more feasible. So further developing 'time markets' — enabling a two-way exchange between people wanting to work on schedules that do not fit the current norms and people who need work done and can accommodate different time preferences — should be a win-win.[38] The challenge, obviously, is to make the market operate fairly.[39]

d. Give the case for a Citizens' Income a proper hearing

Because women have less continuous and more intermittent patterns of paid work, they are penalised by our fragmented, incoherent, and often perverse tax and benefits 'systems', which constrain them from building up decent careers that make proper use of their skills. I put 'systems' in quotation marks and in the plural because there is not a single system, and they are not really systems at all, but ugly baroque structures built up by incessantly adding different components in an increasingly ramshackle Heath Robinson style. The more you move in and out of employment — faithfully obeying the latest injunction to be adaptable, get on your bike, or whatever — the more complicated and difficult your relationship is with these non-systems. One effect is to deter people from aspiring to work at a higher level, or indeed at all. The benefits system costs the state huge amounts to administer in the place I live, the United Kingdom, and from reports it is similar elsewhere.[40] The system often disables individuals, sapping their morale (because it gets things wrong, or punishes them unfairly), and provides perverse incentives that discourage work and encourage cheating.[41]

A Citizens' Income (a form of basic income for all) is designed to remedy exactly these faults. This idea, originating with the State Bonus League in 1918 and now gaining political traction in the United Kingdom, could be central in tackling the effects of the Paula Principle. At its heart is a regular unconditional payment to each individual, simply as a right of citizenship.[42] The payment would not depend on whether the citizen is working or trying to find work; it is always delivered.

Initially, this might strike you as unrealistic. Until quite recently, the idea was indeed on the outer fringes of political thinking. But there are increasingly powerful reasons why it deserves a proper hearing. Proliferating temporary jobs, part-time work, zero-hours contracts, and many other forms of employment mean that the nature of work has changed fundamentally for so many people. And the tax and welfare systems straining to cope are so convoluted, inadequate, and costly that the Citizens' Income (CI) may be an idea whose time has come. The year 2018, a century after it was first floated, would be a suitable time to introduce it.

The CI would cut away the giant hogweed tangles of conditional payments that currently incur such huge administrative and personal costs. It would change the relationship between paid and unpaid work, providing a more solid platform for both. Crucially, from the Paula perspective, it would make it much, much easier for men to follow mosaic careers without being punished; and it would give a far sounder basis for women not in continuous employment to make use of their competences nevertheless. Instead of sliding into marginal positions in the workforce, they could more easily maintain their engagement, and their talents would not be lost.

The CI is controversial, and not yet adequately modelled and tested. Its effects, including what effect it would have on people's propensity to work, are not wholly predictable. The idea of paying people just because they are citizens, without requiring anything from them, is a hard item to sell politically. It need not involve additional public expenditure but could be introduced on a cost-neutral basis by abolishing all the plethora of conditional benefits, though keeping it to this level would not make it high enough to live off. It might have some regressive effects, benefitting people who did not need it, but arguably no more than the current system. In short, as more and more people become aware, or suffer directly, the inadequacies of our current systems, a Citizens' Income, or something like it, begins to come in closer from the distant horizon of what is feasible.

An alternative would be to look for smaller, more focused, measures, such as governmental support for job-sharing or for part-time employment. The problem is that these would just add to the thicket of subsidies; in particular, they would subsidise the low-wage, low-productivity economy. But if robots do indeed take over increasing areas of work, there will inevitably be fewer jobs to go round. And since robots do not spend money, we need ways of maintaining purchasing power, as well as giving people a stake in the economy — which means new mixes of paid and unpaid activity.[43] It all suggests that a full-blown debate on a Citizens' Income would be an important part of changing our work-time culture.[44]

Seeing careers through the lens of development more than of hierarchy

We've been told often that the traditional career is over, along with long-term service with the same employer, and we'll all have to change careers many times. In fact, this seems to be happening rather more slowly than the futurists commonly suggest. Many people still do stick with the same employer for many years, and carry on in the same occupation. What I'm suggesting is a different kind of change: towards mosaic careers that purposively involve lateral and even downward moves, not constrained by a perpetual urge to climb upwards in the hierarchy. *The key definer of career progression should be personal development, not rank*. In other words, what should matter is whether you are growing in the job, not whether you are always moving upwards.

I am well aware that this is a highly normative statement, easy for a man comfortably at the end of his conventional career to make. Moving upwards usually means more money, and for many that is the clincher. But a broader understanding of personal career seems to me to be in line with a more general change in how we measure progress. There is now an immensely important, if still inchoate, rethink underway of how we might define what really gives us wellbeing, away from unquestioning worship of GDP towards a broader set of social and environmental measures.[45] Above a certain level, spending and earning more and more isn't the route to happiness, or even contentment; that's hardly breaking news, but what is striking is how some of our most eminent bean-counters are coming up with different ways of looking at the beans, or measuring progress. Global warming and the impending environmental crisis have much to do with this, but it goes well beyond that.[46]

Just as ever-rising GDP is a poor proxy for national wellbeing, so ever-rising professional ranking is a poor indicator of an individual's wellbeing at work. Lewis Mumford, the great philosopher of technology, offered an incisive and compelling criticism of 'single-direction' thinking many decades ago: 'There is only one efficient speed: faster; only one attractive destination: further away; only one desirable size: bigger; only one rational quantitative goal: more.'[47]

To this we could add: 'And only one desirable career path: vertically upwards.' When Mumford says, 'Today, the notion of progress in a single line without goal or limit seems perhaps the most parochial notion of a very parochial century', he instils in me the hope that dethroning the full-time linear career might be a defining feature of our new century: one where the competences of both women and men can flourish and be recognised appropriately.

Conclusion

This book has its origins in the tension between two trends. On the one hand, there is a steadily increasing gap between women and men in how far they acquire qualifications and skills, at all levels and at every age. Girls do better than boys at school; women do better than men in colleges and universities. This is a remarkably consistent trend across most developed countries. Later in life, women go on adding to their learning in greater numbers than men, by taking part more in adult education generally, and often also in vocational training. This is less clearly established as a universal trend — statistics on adult learning are sadly deficient. But anyone working in adult education, as I have, will confirm it.

On the other hand, the gap between men's and women's careers and relative rewards at work is diminishing. But it is diminishing only slowly and unevenly — and not as steadily nor as fast as the first gap is increasing. The gender pay gap is still there, and progress in reducing it seems to have slowed or even stalled in many countries. It is not just a question of wages. The failure to recognise women's competences fully means that their career paths are often far flatter than should be the case on any meritocratic calculation.

It is this dual dynamic that animates the Paula Principle, and is routinely ignored in the debates about equality at work. Too often the discussion assumes that the magic figure is zero, and that we should be aiming for no differences between women and men in their careers.

I have argued that this aspiration doesn't fit. We are underestimating the effects of the Paula Principle if we think in terms of equality in the simple sense.

Relatedly, I have argued that it is crucial to see the issues raised by the Paula Principle in the context of the full working lives of women and men. These now commonly extend to 45 or 50 years. Again, literal symmetry is not the answer: however much progress is made on parental leave; good, affordable childcare; and social attitudes to sharing child-rearing, women are still more likely to devote more time to bringing up children than men in the third, fourth, and fifth decades of their lives. (I stress 'more likely': it is a matter of probability, combined with choice.) Focusing too tightly on this phase ignores the crucial possibility that some women will resume careers later, with plenty of time to make them successful — if our workplaces and our cultures enable it.

I observed that the Paula Principle currently applies only to countries that have already modernised, in the 20th century understanding of that term. In much of the world, women are still far behind educationally; nearly two out of three of the 750 million who lack basic literacy are women. But it is reasonable to assume that as these countries evolve, women will not only catch up educationally but also overtake men. Changes in culture affect educational opportunities (sometimes negatively, as we see with reactionary fundamentalist regimes that seek to close down girls' schools), and education in turn affects culture, including how people understand differences in what women and men can do. This interaction between education and culture plays out in very varied ways across the globe. Japan and Korea, for example, are arguably the most advanced instances of the Paula Principle. Their overall cultures value education highly, and their women lead the field in qualifications. But their workplace cultures do not value women's competences, so the pay and career gaps remain very large.

Predictably, this is generating tensions within their societies. Hyun-Joo's story in Chapter 7 is a case in point.

It is this cultural, social, and organisational variation that I hope the idea of the Paula Principle will help us to understand better. In Chapter 4, I suggested taking the five PP factors — discrimination and values, caring responsibilities, self-confidence and identity, social capital, and choice — and allocating 20 votes between them according to how important you think they are in explaining why the Paula Principle occurs. You could do this with reference to your own workplace, the industry in which you work, your country as a whole, or just your own experience generally. Then compare it with how friends or colleagues have allocated their votes. If you have nothing to discuss at that point, I'd be amazed.

One quite sobering message is how limited the impact of education can be. I've worked in one form or another of education — mostly with adults — for all of my professional life. Like many of my colleagues, I have indulged in educational boosterism from time to time, promoting learning of all kinds as the best possible form of investment. I still believe wholeheartedly in its value. But the thrust of the argument here is that education and training on their own can only go so far in enabling people to achieve their potential. In the case of enabling women to find fulfilment at work, raising their qualification levels can only get them a certain distance. We need, in short, to be a little bit sceptical about some of the claims for education, and pay far more attention to how the competences signalled by these qualifications are actually recognised and used.

I want to remind you, if it's needed, that the Paula Principle extends to all occupational levels, not just to high-flying professionals. From top-ranking civil servants and engineers to care workers and cleaners, the women who talked to me conveyed the sense that they needed their work to be recognised and valued — not necessarily or even primarily in cash — and they wanted to feel that opportunities to progress were genuinely open. It's true, as Lesley reminded us (Chapter 8), many women want to turn up, work, get paid fairly for what they do, and then go home. Many men are in the same position. But women, in part driven by their superior educational achievement, are increasingly looking to move forwards in a career, even if their notion of a career may not fit the existing norm. The images of what counts as a career are powerful shapers of how we think, and how our workplaces are organised. I have argued that maybe we can start to think of careers less as vertical ladders and more as mosaics that people put together from pieces of quite diverse shapes and sizes. When it becomes commonplace for men to think in those terms, women's opportunities will burgeon.

The dual dynamic between the competence gap and the career gap presents a curious, unfair, and wasteful paradox, which may get more rather than less acute. There is no guarantee that societies and workplaces will take the rational and fair route towards enabling women to realise their potential at work. Nearly 50 years ago, Laurence Peter produced his principle, and there are still plenty of examples of people rising to their level of incompetence. I prefer to be optimistic, and expect the Peter and Paula Principles to fade away together, like twin Cheshire cats.

Notes

Preface

1   As well as difficulties in finding a publisher — it's worth just recording that the book was turned down by more than one publisher on the grounds that a book on this topic by a man would not sell. I'm very fortunate that the quite prolonged search for a publisher led me to Scribe.

Chapter 1

1   George Eliot, *The Mill on the Floss*, Penguin Books, London, 2003 (first published 1860), p. 9. Subsequent quotation in this paragraph, p. 12.

2   ibid., p. 12. Subsequent quotation in this paragraph, p. 16.

3   ibid., p. 32.

4   Winifred Holtby, *South Riding*, Macmillan, New York, 1936, p. 38.

5   ibid., p. 424.

6   The author Winifred Holtby was the close friend of Vera Brittain, whose daughter was Shirley Williams — later to become the UK Secretary of State for Education.

7   Dr Laurence J. Peter and Raymond Hull, *The Peter Principle*, Pan Books, London, 1969.

8   ibid., p. 30 (italics in original).

9   His book is dedicated 'to all those who, working, playing, loving, living and dying at the Level of Incompetence, provided the data for the founding and development of the salutary science of Hierarchology. They saved others: themselves they could not save.'

10 In this book, I shift between several terms — competence, skill, qualification, and so on — that are not identical. Only when I feel the context needs it do I make distinctions between these different terms.

11 'Employment and Labour Market', Office for National Statistics, www.
    ons.gov.uk/employmentandlabourmarket and 'Gender Workplace
    Statistics at a Glance', Workplace Gender Equality Agency, Australian
    Government, August 2016, www.wgea.gov.au/sites/default/files/
    Stats_at_a_Glance.pdf. Most of the specific statistical data in the book
    are from the United Kingdom (where I live) and Australia (where this
    book is also published), but they usually apply broadly to other OECD
    countries.

12 For further discussion of this point, see for example Alison Wolf, *The
    XX Factor: how working women are creating a new society*, Profile Books,
    London, 2013.

13 See for recent examples Royal Society of Edinburgh, *Tapping All Our
    Talents: women in science, technology, engineering, and mathematics —
    a strategy for Scotland*, Edinburgh, 2012, https://www.royalsoced.org.uk/
    cms/files/advice-papers/inquiry/women_in_stem/tapping_talents.pdf;
    and for the international picture OECD, *Closing the Gender Gap: act now*,
    OECD Publishing, 2012, http://www.oecd.org/gender/closingthegap.htm

14 The statistics in this paragraph are drawn from UK Women & Work
    Commission, *Shaping a Fairer Future*, 2006, p. 6; Kristen Barsh
    and Lareina Yee, *Unlocking the Full Potential of Women in the US
    Economy*, McKinsey Global Institute, 2011, http://www.mckinsey.
    com/womenineconomy; and Jonathan Woetzel et al., *How Advancing
    Women's Equality Can Add $12 Trillion to Global Growth*, McKinsey
    Global Institute, 2015, http://www.mckinsey.com/global-themes/
    employment-and-growth/how-advancing-womens-equality-can-add-
    12-trillion-to-global-growth

15 Government Equalities Office, 'Closing the Gender Pay Gap', 2015,
    https://www.gov.uk/government/uploads/system/uploads/attachment_
    data/file/450878/Gender_Pay_Gap_Consultation.pdf

16 See, for example, Chapter 11 in Iris Bohnet, *What Works: gender equality
    by design*, Harvard University Press, Cambridge, 2016.

17 High Pay Centre, *The New Closed Shop: who's deciding on pay?*, 2012,
    http://highpaycentre.org/files/hpc_dp_remco.pdf

18 Janet Russell's 'The Secretary's Song', which appears on the CD
    Gathering the Fragments, captures this with acerbity. The song can be

viewed on YouTube: https://www.youtube.com/watch?v=ht0teFoHdMo
(Thanks to Rosemary Milne for pointing me to this song.)

From an earlier time, *Middlemarch* is a painful illustration of
contrasting competences within a tight hierarchy. The heroine Dorothea
chooses to marry the dry-stick Casaubon. In an act of intellectual self-
abasement, she, a highly intelligent young woman, submits herself to his
supposedly scholarly (and, as it happens, futile) demands.

19 One calculation for the European Union's work on science and
gender showed that literally equalising the numbers of male and
female professors in physical and chemical sciences in France would
mean reducing the number of male professors by 1,576 — and even
in humanities, by 1,124. See Rosetta Palomba, 'Women Scientists:
guidelines for statistical indicators', cited in Expert Working Group on
Women and Science, *Science Policies in the European Union: promoting
excellence through mainstreaming gender quality*, European Commission,
2000, p. 76. Such a dramatic academic cull remains purely hypothetical.

20 See Sheryl Sandberg, *Lean In: women, work, and the will to lead*, Knopf
Doubleday, New York, 2013.

21 This despite the Dilbert Principle: 'Leadership is nature's way of
removing morons from the productive flow'; that is, organisations
promote people to management positions to get them out of the way
of those doing the real work.

Chapter 2

1 For example, *Man-Made: why so few women are in positions of power*,
by Eva Tutchell and John Edmonds, is a well-argued case for greater
gender equality, but it assumes — without discussion — that this is
to be thought of as absolute numerical equality.

2 Willy Russell, *Educating Rita*, Bloomsbury, London, 2007 (first published
1981), p. 183.

3 ibid., p. 171.

4 ibid., p. 228.

5 Carrie Harding et al., *Community Learning Learner Survey Report*,
Department for Business, Innovation, and Skills, BIS Research Paper
108, 2013. One analysis puts female participation in all three forms of

adult learning — formal education, job-related training, and leisure education — already ahead in 1999, and continuing to be ahead in 2002. This is after controlling for age, qualifications, and whether the person was employed. See Geoff Mason, *Adult Education in Decline? Recent Evidence at UK National and City-region Level*, Centre for Learning and Life Chances in Knowledge Economies and Societies, Institute of London, Research Paper 15, 2010, p. 19.

6 European Commission, *Education and Training Monitor 2012*, Publications Office of the European Union, Table 8.1.

7 OECD, *Education at a Glance 2014*, OECD Publishing, 2014, Table 2.4, http://www.oecd.org/edu/Education-at-a-Glance-2014.pdf

8 ibid.

9 OECD, *Closing the Gender Gap*, op. cit., p. 100.

10 Michael Barber et al., *An Avalanche is Coming: higher education and the revolution ahead*, Institute for Public Policy Research, 2013, p. 15.

11 Helen Beebee and Jenny Saul, *Women in Philosophy in the UK*, British Philosophical Association and the Society of Women in Philosophy UK, 2011, http://www.bpa.ac.uk/uploads/2011/02/BPA_Report_Women_In_Philosophy.pdf

12 See Katrina Hutchison and Fiona Jenkins (eds), *Women in Philosophy: who needs to change?*, Oxford University Press, Oxford, 2015, plus an interesting review of the book by David Papineau, *Times Literary Supplement*, 15 July 2015, http://www.davidpapineau.co.uk/uploads/1/8/5/5/18551740/women_in_philosophy_tls_proofs.pdf

13 Figures from Department for Education, 'A Level and Other Level 3 Results: 2014 to 2015 (provisional)', 2015, https://www.gov.uk/government/statistics/a-level-and-other-level-3-results-2014-to-2015-provisional

14 See Pietro Patrignani and Gavin Conlon, 'The Long-term Effects of Vocational Qualifications on Labour Market Outcomes', Department for Business Innovation and Skills, DBIS Research Paper 47, 2011, https://www.gov.uk/government/uploads/system/uploads/attachment_data/file/32326/11-1035-long-term-effect-of-vocational-qualifications.pdf.

15 'Introduction — Students 2014/15', Higher Education Statistics Agency, 2016, https://www.hesa.ac.uk/data-and-analysis/publications/students-2014-15/introduction

16 ibid.

17 Almost all the trends I quote are valid for the United Kingdom as a whole. But Scotland and Northern Ireland have distinctive education systems, and for these crossover points I have needed to separate out the figures for England and Wales.

18 See the Platform for Action from the United Nations Fourth World Conference on Women, held in Beijing, China, in September 1995, at http://www.un.org/womenwatch/daw/beijing/platform/educa.htm

19 One index of how widely recognised it is that lack of education is a crucial brake on progress is the way in which aid money is allocated: in 2009/10, on average 60% of aid to education in poorer countries from all the OECD countries (excluding the United States) was directed specifically to achieving greater gender equality in education, notably in Sub-Saharan Africa.

20 National Institute of Adult Continuing Education, *Women's Right to Literacy: advocating women's right to access learning literacy through international development*, 2012, http://www.learningandwork.org.uk/ sites/niace_en/files/document-downloads/womensrighttoliteracy_web.pdf

21 See *3rd Global Report on Adult Learning and Education: the impact of adult learning and education on health and well-being; employment and the labour market; and social, civic, and community life*, UNESCO Institute for Lifelong Learning, 2016, https://uil.unesco.org/system/files/grale-3.pdf

22 Australian Bureau of Statistics, 'Australia's Workers: education and workplace training', 2010, http://www.abs.gov.au/AUSSTATS/abs@.nsf/ Lookup/4102.0Main+Features60Sep+2010

23 Office for National Statistics, 'EMP15: Job-related Training Received by Employees', June–August 2016, https://www.ons.gov.uk/employmentandlabourmarket/ peopleinwork/employmentandemployeetypes/datasets/ jobrelatedtrainingreceivedbyemployeesemp15

24 Alan Felstead et al., *Skills at Work, 1986 to 2006*, ESRC Centre on Skills, Knowledge, and Organisational Performance, 2007, p.84.

25 Sin Yi Cheung and Stephen McKay, *Training and Progression in the Labour Market*, Department for Work and Pensions, Research Report No. 680, 2010, Fig. 2.2.

26 This is one of a number of evident generalisations I make in this book. Some are supported by evidence. I draw more on my conversations and on experience than on research, and invite disproof.

27 Sin Yi Cheung and Stephen McKay, *Training and Progression in the Labour Market*, op. cit., Fig 2.5. I'm told also (for example, by researcher Satya Brink, in relation to Canada) that more women than men fund their own training, but I have no information on how widespread this is.

28 Francis Green et al., *Training in Britain: first findings from the Skills and Employment Survey 2012*, Centre for Learning and Life Chances in Knowledge Economies and Societies, Institute of Education, London, 2013, http://www.cardiff.ac.uk/__data/assets/pdf_file/0018/118701/2.-Training-in-Britain-mini-report.pdf

Chapter 3

1 Dorothy Whipple, *High Wages*, Persephone Books, London, 2009 (first published 1930), p. 153.

2 That nightmarish prospect was cleverly satirised by Michael Young in his 1960s classic, *The Rise of the Meritocracy*. Young illuminated the dangers of relying too much on 'merit', especially when inequality is unconstrained. Perhaps sadly, his original concept of meritocracy, drained of its satirical bite, has come to be used as an unambiguously desirable goal.

3 *The Invisible Workforce: employment practices in the cleaning sector*, Equality and Human Rights Commission, 2014, https://www.equalityhumanrights.com/en/publication-download/invisible-workforce-employment-practices-cleaning-sector

4 See a telling blog by Athene Donald, herself an eminent promoter of women's academic opportunities, arguing against unrealistic expectations that undermine positive initiatives (in this case on women's representation in science): 'Attacks on the Royal Society Miss the Point', *Athene Donald's Blog*, 12 May 2014, http://occamstypewriter.org/athenedonald/2014/05/12/attacks-on-the-royal-society-miss-the-point

5 Carolyn G. Heilbrun, *Writing a Woman's Life*, Women's Press, London, 1989, p. 84. See also Virginia Valian, *Why So Slow?*, The MIT Press, Cambridge, 1997; the book is strongly argued, but I don't think Valian ever actually defines what 'slow' is, or 'fast' would be.

6   OECD, 'Gender Wage Gap', 2016, http://www.oecd.org/gender/data/ genderwagegap.htm

7   See 'Closing the Gender Pay Gap', Government Equalities Office, 2016, https://www.gov.uk/government/uploads/system/uploads/attachment_ data/file/500087/Government_response_-_Closing_the_Gender_Pay_ Gap.pdf

8   John Hills et al., 'An Anatomy of Economic Inequality in the UK', Government Equalities Office, 2010, http://sticerd.lse.ac.uk/case/_new/ publications/NEP.asp. Box 10.1 specifically discusses different ways of measuring pay inequality. I have reproduced Table 10A from Box 10.1. The data in Table 10A is drawn from the Labour Force Survey 2006–8.

9   'Annual Survey of Hours and Earnings Statistical Bulletins: 2015 provisional results', Office of National Statistics, 2015, http://www.ons.gov.uk/employmentandlabourmarket/ peopleinwork/earningsandworkinghours/bulletins/ annualsurveyofhoursandearnings/2015provisionalresults

10 UK statistic: 'The State of Pay: High Pay Centre briefing on executive pay', High Pay Centre, 2015, http://highpaycentre.org/files/State_of_ Pay_Aug_2015.pdf; US statistic: quoted in Merryn Somerset Webb, 'How Excessive Executive Pay Scrimps Your Returns', *Financial Times*, 27 April 2013, http://www.ft.com/cms/s/0/68d53870-ae59-11e2-bdfd-00144feabdc0.html?siteedition=intl#axzz4Lo4t9l00.

11 Peter Swan, 'CEO Pay Study Shows How Much Australians Tolerate Inequality', *The Conversation*, 26 September 2014, http:// theconversation.com/ceo-pay-study-shows-how-much-australians-tolerate-inequality-32140

12 Thomas Piketty, *Capital in the 21st Century*, Harvard University Press, Massachusetts, 2013.

13 Alice Sullivan et al., 'Single Sex Schooling and Labour Market Outcomes', *Oxford Review of Education*, volume 37, issue 3, 2011, pp. 311–32.

14 Kate Purcell et al., 'Transitions into Employment, Further Study and Other Outcomes: the Futuretrack Stage 4 report', Warwick University Institute for Employment Research, 2012, Fig. 5.8.

15 Jermaine Haughton, 'Most Female Managers Would Have to Work Up to 80 to Get Equal Pay', Chartered Management Institute, 19 August 2014,

http://www.managers.org.uk/insights/news/2014/august/most-female-managers-would-have-to-work-up-to-80-to-get-equal-pay

16 Kate Purcell and Peter Elias, 'Achieving Equality in the Knowledge Economy', in Jacqueline Scott et al. (eds), *Women and Employment: changing lives and new challenges*, Ed Elgar, Cheltenham, 2008, pp. 19–53.

17 Calculated from Office of National Statistics, 'Annual Survey of Hours and Earnings: 2013 provisional results', Office of National Statistics, 2013, Table 12, http://www.ons.gov.uk/ons/dcp171778_335027.pdf

18 'Gender Pay Gap Statistics', Workplace Gender Equality Agency, August 2014, https://www.wgea.gov.au/sites/default/files/Gender_Pay_Gap_factsheet.pdf

19 See Glen Elder's *Children of the Great Depression*, which shows how the generation born in the United States in the ruinously depressed conditions of the 1920s was affected by where it surfaced in the ebb and flow of history.

20 Alison Wolf, *The XX Factor*, op. cit.

21 United Nations, 'The Rise of the South: human progress in a diverse world', *Human Development Report 2013*, p. 88.

22 OECD, 'Closing the Gender Gap', op. cit., p. 101.

23 Statistics in this paragraph: biggest wage gap, ibid., p. 168; work rates for South Korean women, Terri Kim, 'Globalization and Higher Education in South Korea: towards ethnocentric internationalization or global commercialization of higher education?' in Roger King et al. (eds), *Handbook of Globalization and Higher Education*, Edward Elgar, Cheltenham, 2011, pp. 286–305; women managers and social attitudes, OECD, 'Closing the Gender Gap', op. cit., p. 35.

24 'UK Labour Market: March 2016', Office of National Statistics, 2016, http://www.ons.gov.uk/employmentandlabourmarket/peopleinwork/employmentandemployeetypes/bulletins/uklabourmarket/march2016

25 'LFS by Sex and Age — Indicators: employment-population ratios', OECD.Stat, 2016, http://stats.oecd.org/Index.aspx?QueryId=64196

26 Taken from the excellent site Flip Chart Fairy Tales. The quotation appears in the post 'A Few Part-time Workers Get Good Rates. Most Don't', 21 June 2012, https://flipchartfairytales.wordpress.com/

2012/06/21/a-few-part-time-workers-get-good-rates-most-dont/

27 Carol Shields, *The Stone Diaries*, Fourth Estate, London, 1994, pp. 226, 229.

28 Erzsebet Bukodi et al., 'Changing Career Trajectories of Women and Men Across Time', in Jacqueline Scott et al. (eds), *Gendered Lives: gender inequalities in production and reproduction*, Edward Elgar, Cheltenham, 2012, p. 61.

29 A seminal discussion is George Lakoff and Mark Johnson, *Metaphors We Live By*, University of Chicago Press, Chicago, 1980.

30 Michelle K. Ryan et al., *The Glass Cliff: precariousness beyond the glass ceiling*, Chartered Institute of Personnel and Development, London, 2007. See also http://psychology.exeter.ac.uk/research/glasscliff

31 Sue Unerman & Kathryn Jacob, The Glass Wall – success strategies for women at work – and businesses that mean business, Profile Books 2016."

32 Alice H. Eagly and Linda L. Carli, *Through the Labyrinth: the truth about how women become leaders*, Harvard Business Press, Boston, 2007.

33 The Royal Society, 'The Scientific Century: securing our future prosperity', 2010, London, p. 14. There are some imaginative initiatives designed to counter this process (often evocatively titled, such as the Athena SWAN Charter, or Project Juno, the Institute of Physics Juno Championship).

34 Satya Brink, in a personal communication, makes it clear that she does not like the use of the term 'convergence' — it suggests a more rapid pace of change than is happening. I take her point, but I think of convergence as a process, open to criticism for being too slow. But see also Chapter 9, where I argue that we need to stop assuming that the goal is for women's careers to converge with men's, and think instead of promoting 'reverse convergence'.

Chapter 4

1 This is an interesting pairing for another reason: egalitarian Sweden has an exceptionally high level of occupational segregation — that is, women and men show a strong tendency to cluster in different occupations — while Saudi Arabia has a very high level of female graduates but little choice for them in the way of jobs.

2 The bar was removed for teachers and in the BBC in 1944, and in the

civil service, most local governments, and the post office in 1954. In certain organisations — including some union offices — the bar survived into the 1960s. When I first began teaching, in 1972, the school had only recently abandoned the rule that a woman should ask the head teacher for permission to carry on teaching after getting married.

3   Peter Searle, 'There's No Good Reason For This Inequality', *Times Higher Education*, 30 June 2011, https://www.timeshighereducation.com/features/theres-no-good-reason-for-this-inequality/416651.article

4   Transcript of oral evidence from Fiona Woolf, cited in 'Women in the Workplace: first report of session 2013–14', volume 1, House of Commons Business, Innovation and Skills Committee, 11 June 2013, p. 30.

5   Kate Purcell et al., 'Transitions into Employment, Further Study, and Other Outcomes', op. cit., Fig. 5.8. Here is the view of Supreme Court judge Jonathan Sumption on how fast progress is likely to be: 'You've got to be patient. The change in the status and achievements of women in our society, not just in the law but generally, is an enormous cultural change that has happened over the last 50 years or so. It has to happen naturally. It will happen naturally. But in the history of a society like ours, 50 years is a very short time.' There are, he felt, dangers in rushing things. 'We have got to be very careful not to do things at a speed which will make male candidates feel that the cards are stacked against them. If we do that, we will find that male candidates don't apply in the right numbers.' See 'Minding the Gap', *The Paula Principle*, 14 October 2015, http://www.paulaprinciple.com/minding-the-gap/

6   Noreena Hertz, 'Women and Banks: are female customers facing discrimination?', Institute for Public Policy Research, 2011, http://www.ippr.org/publications/women-and-banks-are-female-customers-facing-discrimination

7   'National Gender Pay Gap at Record High of 18.8%', Workplace Gender Equality Agency, 2015, https://www.wgea.gov.au/news-and-media/national-gender-pay-gap-record-high-188 and Workplace Gender Equality Agency Data Explorer, http://data.wgea.gov.au/comparison/?id1=115&id2=114

8   Kate Eastman, 'Sex Discrimination in the Legal Profession', *UNSW Law Journal*, volume 27, number 3, p. 867.

9   OECD, 'Closing the Gender Gap', op. cit., p. 232.

10   This holds even more strongly for non-graduates than graduates. See
     Conor D'Arcy and David Finch, 'Finding Your Routes: non-graduate
     pathways in the UK labour market', Resolution Foundation, 2016,
     http://www.resolutionfoundation.org/publications/finding-your-routes-
     non-graduate-pathways-in-the-uks-labour-market

11   'Trends in the Netherlands 2015', Statistics Netherlands, 2015,
     http://investinholland.com/nfia_media/2015/05/2015-Trends-in-the-
     Netherlands-web.pdf

12   Daniel Kahneman, *Thinking Fast and Slow*, Penguin, London, 2011.

13   Christine Wennerås and Agnes Wold, 'Nepotism and Sexism in Peer
     Review,' *Nature*, volume 347, 1997, pp. 341–3. The study is cited in a
     report from the European Union's Expert Working Group on Women
     and Science, 'Science Policies in the European Union', op. cit. It also
     describes other examples of similar bias, in Germany, the Netherlands,
     and the United Kingdom, including in foundations and scientific bodies
     whose watchword is scientific objectivity.

14   Corinne Moss-Racusin et al., 'Science Faculty's Subtle Gender Biases
     Favor Male Students', *Proceedings of the National Academies of Sciences
     of the United States of America*, volume 109, issue 41, 2012, pp. 16474–9.

15   There is also shocking evidence on the extent and nature of sexual
     harassment in schools. This is arguably a form of discrimination, though
     exactly how to classify it is not the main issue. See Chapter 2 of Kat
     Banyard's *The Equality Illusion*, London, Faber
     & Faber, 2010.

16   Comment from my older daughter: 'I don't know anybody who has
     gained anything from visiting a careers office!'

17   *Apprenticeship Pay Survey 2014*, Research Paper 207, Department of
     Business, Innovation & Skills, 2014, Table 3.11; Australian statistics:
     'Hairdresser Fact Sheet', ANZSCO 3911–11, Australian Government
     Department of Employment, 2015, https://docs.employment.gov.au/
     system/files/doc/other/391111hairdresseraus_2.pdf and 'Electricians',
     Open Universities Australia, 2015, https://www.open.edu.au/careers/
     construction/electricians. Pay rates calculated by the government's Pay
     and Conditions Tool: https://calculate.fairwork.gov.au

18 'Making Apprenticeships Work for Young Women', Young Women's Trust, 2016, p. 4.

19 A particular initiative that has had considerable impact in the United Kingdom is the 30% Club, launched to bring about that level of women non-executive directors by 2015. See http://30percentclub.org

20 In 2016, the Scottish Funding Council set a sector-wide target to ensure that 'no subject has an extreme gender imbalance', defined as less than 25% of one gender, by 2030. See 'Gender Action Plan: interim report', Scottish Funding Council, Edinburgh, February 2016, p. 14. This seems to me a good pragmatic goal, which allows childcare and computing to be brought into the same frame. Cited in Nick Hillman and Nicholas Robinson, 'Boys to Men: the underachievement of young men in higher education — and how to start tackling it', Higher Education Policy Institute Report 84, 2016, http://www.hepi.ac.uk/wp-content/uploads/2016/05/Boys-to-Men.pdf

21 Penelope, the main character in Nina Bawden's *Afternoon of a Good Woman*, is a magistrate. She explains to her nephew what this means to her: 'It's normal to enjoy having a hand in running things ... Of course I like feeling important but I don't think I'm corrupted by it. In fact, quite the opposite. I never expected much, or thought much of myself, and it's done me good these last eight years or so to feel — well — a person of consequence.' She pulls a face to show that she is not too solemn about it (p. 150).

22 Jane Sims, 'When Will Workplace Sexism Go Away?', *People Management*, 28 June 2016, http://www.cipd.co.uk/pm/peoplemanagement/b/weblog/archive/2016/06/28/why-is-work-still-sexist.aspx

23 IFF Research, 'Pregnancy and Maternity-related Discrimination and Disadvantage', Equalities and Human Rights Commission, BIS Research Paper No. 235, 2016.

24 Diann Rodgers-Healey, 'We Must Do Better to Curb Discrimination Against Working Parents', *The Conversation*, 28 July 2014, http://theconversation.com/we-must-do-better-to-curb-discrimination-against-working-parents-29696. The article summarises data from the national review 'Supporting Working Parents: pregnancy and return to work', Human Rights Commission, 2014.

25 'A recent study of the National Bureau of Economic Research in the United States found "robust" evidence based on looking at more than 40,000 job applications of age discrimination in hiring female candidates and "considerably less evidence" for age discrimination against male candidates.' Evidence from the Employment Lawyers Association to the House of Commons Select Committee on Women and Equality, in 'Gender Pay Gap: second report of session 2015–16', 2016, note 155.

26 Richard Desjardins and Kjell Rubenson, 'An Analysis of Skill Mismatch Using Direct Measures of Skills', OECD Education Working Paper 63, 2011, p. 30. The analysis is of the Adult Literacy and Lifeskills Survey, a major comparative study on literacy and numeracy carried out between 2003 and 2008.

27 Damian Grimshaw and Jill Rubery, 'Undervaluing Women's Work', Research Paper 53, European Work and Employment Research Centre, University of Manchester, 2007, p. 59.

28 It is at the heart of the philosopher-economist Amartya Sen's subtle notion of capability, which has been highly influential on thinking about global inequalities.

Chapter 5

1 Alison Wolf, *The XX Factor*, op. cit., Ch. 11.

2 Shirley Dex et al., 'Changes in Women's Occupations and Occupational Mobility Over 25 Years', in Jacqueline Scott et al. (eds), *Women and Employment*, op. cit.

3 Erzsebet Bukodi et al., 'Changing Career Trajectories of Women and Men Across Time', op. cit. But see Rebecca Asher's account of the stress costs, as well as career penalties, in *Shattered: modern motherhood and the illusion of equality*, Harvill Secker, London, 2011.

4 Jean Martin and Ceridwen Roberts, 'Putting Women on the Research Agenda: the 1980 Women and Employment Survey', in Jacqueline Scott et al. (eds), *Women and Employment*, op. cit.

5 Daisy Sands, 'The Impact of Austerity on Women', Fawcett Society Policy Briefing, 2012, http://www.fawcettsociety.org.uk/wp-content/uploads/2013/02/The-Impact-of-Austerity-on-Women-19th-March-2012.pdf

6   'Early Childhood and Child Care in Summary: March quarter 2015',
    Australian Government Department of Education and Training,
    2015, p. 12.

7   Jill Rutter and Katherine Stocker, 'Childcare Costs in 2014', Family
    and Childcare Trust, 2014, https://www.lincolnshire.gov.uk/
    Download/65386

8   See Vidhya Alakeson and Alex Hurrell, 'Paying the Costs of Childcare',
    Resolution Foundation, 2012, http://www.resolutionfoundation.org/
    wp-content/uploads/2014/08/The_costs_of_childcare_after_housing_
    costs_1.pdf

9   Becky's story is taken from the *Gingerbread* website, cited in Daisy Sands,
    'The Impact of Austerity on Women', p. 32. It refers to proposed changes
    in the tax credit arrangements to be implemented in 2013, but the central
    message remains the same.

10 Interestingly, in the light of its reputation for technological competence,
    only about 16% of Germany's computer-science graduates are women,
    well below the OECD average of just under 20%. This figure has in fact
    been declining in recent years.

11 Allison Pearson's *I Don't Know How She Does It* (Vintage, London, 2003)
    is a hilarious but telling account of such juggling.

12 Kayte Lawton et al., 'The Condition of Britain: strategies for social
    renewal', Institute of Public Policy Research, London, 2014, p. 221.

13 Robert Beasley, 'Attendance Allowance, Disability Living Allowance,
    and Carer's Allowance: retrospective equality impact assessment',
    Welfare and Wellbeing Group, http://webarchive.nationalarchives.gov.
    uk/20130128102031/http:/www.dwp.gov.uk/docs/aa-dla-ca.pdf

14 OECD, 'Closing the Gender Gap', op. cit., p. 202.

15 Alexandra Heron, 'Who Cares?: employer and employee responses to
    employee eldercare responsibilities', Women & Work Research Group,
    University of Sydney Business School, keynote address to NSW Carers
    Association Conference on 22 May 2015. Data is drawn from the 2012
    Australian Bureau of Statistics Disability, Ageing and Carers Survey,
    published 2013.

16 Claire Messud, *The Woman Upstairs*, Virago, London, 2013, pp. 62–3.

Chapter 6

1 Ann Oakley, *The Sociology of Housework*, Martin Robertson, London, 1974.

2 See Linda Babcock and Sara Laschever, *Women Don't Ask: negotiation and the gender divide*, Bantam Books, New York, 2007 for extensive evidence.

3 Eva Tutchell and John Edmonds quote a headhunter on the same point: 'Women seem to search for the one requirement that they are uncertain about and then assume that a single deficiency will rule them out. If there are 18 requirements and a woman has 17, I find myself talking all the time about the solitary requirement she thinks she cannot meet.' (*Man-Made*, op. cit., p. 54).

4 Katty Kay and Claire Shipman, *The Confidence Code: the science and art of self-assurance — what women should know*, HarperCollins, New York, 2014.

5 David Brooks, 'The Problem with Confidence', *New York Times*, 12 May 2014, http://www.nytimes.com/2014/05/13/opinion/brooks-the-problem-with-confidence.html

6 See http://www.librinova.com/librairie/soleine-leprince-ringuet/carrieres-a-ciel-ouvert

7 Virginia Woolf was there first: 'All these relationships between women, I thought, rapidly recalling the splendid gallery of fictitious women, are too simple ... And I tried to remember any case in the course of my reading where two women are represented as friends ... They are now and then mothers and daughters. But almost without exception they are shown in their relation to men. It was strange to think that all the great women of fiction were, until Jane Austen's day, not only seen by the other sex, but seen only in relation to the other sex. And how small a part of a woman's life is that ...' *A Room of One's Own*, The Hogarth Press, London, 1929, Ch. 5.

8 James Côté, 'Sociological Perspectives on Identity Formation: the culture–identity link and identity capital', *Journal of Adolescence*, volume 19, issue 5, 1996, pp. 417–28.

9 Tom Schuller et al., *The Benefits of Learning*, RoutledgeFalmer, London, 2004.

10 See Linda Babcock and Sara Laschever, *Women Don't Ask*, op. cit.

11 'Pay Progression: understanding the barriers for the lowest paid', Chartered Institute for Personnel and Development, London, 2014, p. 27.

12 See for example Alice H. Eagly and Linda L. Carli, *Through the Labyrinth*, op. cit., p. 104, and Deborah Tannen's work on language and gender, as in *You Just Don't Understand: women and men in conversation*, Ballantine Books, New York, 1990. See also a great little 'ad' on labels: https://www.youtube.com/watch?v=-K2kfgW7708

13 Thanks to Rosemary Milne for pointing me to this quotation.

Chapter 7

1 This has become known as the Miss Triggs phenomenon, named after a stiletto-sharp *Punch* cartoon by Riana Duncan. It features a boardroom; there are only men round the table except for the bespectacled secretary taking notes. The chairman is captioned as saying: 'That's an excellent suggestion, Miss Triggs. Perhaps one of the men here would like to make it?'

2 Psychologist Simon Baron-Cohen makes the case for a distinction between an empathising female brain and a systemising male brain.

3 Mary McCarthy, *The Group*, Virago Books, London, 2009 (first published 1963), p. vii. Quotation in subsequent paragraph ibid., p. 229.

4 The strongest early usage was by a female urbanist Jane Jacobs, who wrote beautifully about social capital's place in Chicago streetlife. For Putnam's popularisation of the term, see Robert Putnam, 'Bowling Alone: America's declining social capital', *Journal of Democracy*, volume 6, issue 1, 1995, pp. 65–78. Also see more recently *American Grace: how religion divides and unites us* (Simon & Schuster, New York, 2010), where Putnam argues controversially that communities that are more than usually heterogeneous ethnically tend to have lower levels of social capital.

5 Apparently bowling clubs elsewhere, for example in the United Kingdom, are flourishing. Thanks to Sue Fyvel for pointing this out.

6 Originally developed by Michael Woolcock: see 'Social Capital and Economic Development: towards a theoretical synthesis and policy framework', *Theory and Society*, volume 27, issue 2, 1998, pp. 151–208.

7   Paul Seabright, *The War Between the Sexes*, Princeton University Press, Princeton, 2013, p. 133. The seminal study on 'homophily' was carried out in the advertising industry. See Herminia Ibarra, 'Homophily and Differential Returns: sex differences in network structure and access in an advertising firm', *Administrative Science Quarterly*, volume 37, number 3, 1992, pp. 422–47.

8   Contrast her response with this, reported in a study of another Asian culture: 'At Daigo life insurance, Tami, a 38-year-old manager, attained her assigned goal of $50 million in sales in 12 months. Tami joined in with after-work drinking sessions with her male bosses every day and played golf every weekend. She described attending hostess clubs with upper managers and their clients as enjoyable. In contrast, Tami explicitly expressed her annoyance with female culture in the company. "Women cry. Women eat so slow and so little. I feel very exhausted when I talk with women."' In Kumiko Nemoto, 'When Culture Resists Progress: masculine organisational culture and its impact on the vertical segregation of women in Japanese companies', *Work, Employment, and Society*, volume 29, issue 1, 2013, pp. 153–69. I find it hard to believe that Tami is comfortable in her skin, but how are we to know?

9   John Field and I once looked at why adults in both Scotland and Northern Ireland, which pride themselves on having better schooling results than England, take part less often in adult education and training. This is the opposite of what you would expect, as success at school normally strengthens people's motivation to take part in adult education. Part of the answer lay in the 'tall-poppy syndrome': in both cultures, there was a perception that once you had had your chance at school you should not think about trying to better yourself and move up. Individuals who may have harboured aspirations to improve themselves encountered resistance from their own peers. See John Field and Tom Schuller, 'Networks, Norms, and Trust: explaining patterns of lifelong learning in Scotland and Northern Ireland', in Frank Coffield (ed.), *Differing Visions of the Learning Society: volume 2*, Policy Press, Bristol, 2000, pp. 95–118.

Chapter 8

1 Quoted by Tony Wright, 'The Queen's Abu Hamza Intervention Could Have Serious Consequences', *The Guardian*, 26 September 2012, https://www.theguardian.com/commentisfree/2012/sep/26/monarchs-and-meddling-the-queen

2 Richard H. Thaler and Cass R. Sunstein, *Nudge: improving decisions about health, wealth, and happiness*, Penguin Books, New York, 2009; Daniel Kahneman, *Thinking Fast and Slow*, op. cit.

3 Barry Schwartz, *The Paradox of Choice: why more is less*, New York, Harper Perennial, 2004.

4 As an aside, it is quite common practice for people to use job offers from another university to accelerate their promotion in their existing university. Men, as stronger negotiators, do this more than women. See Linda Babcock and Sara Laschever, *Women Don't Ask*, op. cit., passim.

5 Tom Stoppard, *Rosencrantz and Guildenstern Are Dead*, Faber & Faber, London, 1967, Act 2, p. 59.

6 Satya Brink has pointed out to me that this can be used as an excuse for not promoting a woman, and selling the decision to her: 'This is the post-job-interview statement women hear a lot: *You are such a good X. Why would you want to do something else?* Perhaps it is said so often, you end up believing it. I have rarely heard men saying that they were advised this way. This would be a positive cure for the Peter Principle, on the other hand.'

7 In France, President Sarkozy set up a star-studded commission to propose different ways of measuring economic and social progress; see Joseph Stiglitz et al., 'Report of the Commission on the Measurement of Economic Performance and Social Progress', 2009, http://www.stiglitz-sen-fitoussi.fr/documents/rapport_anglais.pdf. This has been followed by a similar high-level Enquetekommission in Germany; see Anke Hassel, 'Creating a System of Well-being Warning Lights', Policy Network, 2013, http://www.policy-network.net/pno_detail.aspx?ID=4369. See also Robert and Edward Skidelsky, *How Much is Enough?*, Allen Lane, London, 2012.

8 'Le mariage est la seule carrière des femmes; les hommes ont trente-six chances, la femme n'en a qu'une, le zero, comme à la banque.' Simone de Beauvoir, *Le Deuxième Sexe*, Folio Essais (Book 37), 1949, p. 114.

9   Rebecca Asher, *Shattered*, op. cit., p. 180.

10   Hazel Rowley, *Tete-a-Tete: the lives and loves of Simone de Beauvoir and Jean-Paul Sartre*, Vintage Books, London, 2007, p. 195.

11   Martha Nussbaum, *Women and Human Development: the capabilities approach*, Cambridge University Press, Cambridge, 2000, p. 114.

12   Catherine Hakim, *Work–Lifestyle Choices in the 21st Century: preference theory*, Oxford University Press, Oxford, 2000, p. 200 and pp. 273–4.

13   See for example Susan Macrae, 'Constraints and Choices in Mothers' Employment Careers', *British Journal of Sociology*, volume 54, issue 3, pp. 317–8.

14   See Tania Burkhardt on discretionary time, in Anna Coote (ed.), *A New Economics of Time*, New Economics Foundation, 2013.

15   Charlotta Magnusson, *Mind the Gap: essays on explanations of gender wage inequality*, The Swedish Institute for Social Research, Stockholm University, 2010.

16   Anne-Marie Slaughter points out that in the United States, 'eds and meds' are also the jobs that remain in parts of the country where manufacturing has disappeared. They are, she says, decent jobs, but traditionally less valued and paid less. Anne-Marie Slaughter, *Unfinished Business: women, men, work, and family*, OneWorld, London, 2015, p. 93.

17   Francis Green, 'Is Britain Such a Bad Place to Work?', LLAKES Research Paper 40, Institute of Education, London, 2013.

18   Vidhya Alakeson, 'The Price of Motherhood: women and part-time work', Resolution Foundation, 2012, p. 5.

19   In 1968, women's employment contributed only 11% of the average lower-to-middle-income household income, and men's contributed 71%; today, the respective figures are 24% and 40%. Matthew Whitaker, 'Squeezed Britain in 2013', Resolution Foundation, 2013, p. 20.

Chapter 9

1   Virginia Woolf, *Three Guineas*, Penguin Classics, London, 2000 (first published 1938), p. 119.

2   Carol Tavris, *The Mismeasure of Woman: why women are not the better sex, the inferior sex, or the opposite sex*, Touchstone Books, New York, 1992.

3 'Why can't a woman / Be more like a man ...' from Lerner and Loewe's *My Fair Lady*, Penguin, New York, 1975 (first published 1956).

4 Francis Green, 'Is Britain Such a Bad Place to Work?', op. cit. UK male full-time employees work the longest hours in the European Union. When all categories are included, British men are ninth. Female full-timers are ninth, and part-timers 23rd, in their leagues.

5 Claudia Goldin, presidential address to the American Economic Association, 2014. See Claudia Goldin, 'A Grand Gender Convergence: its last chapter', *American Economic Review*, volume 104, issue 4, 2014, pp. 1091–119.

6 Gaby Hinsliff, *Half a Wife: the working family's guide to getting a life back*, Vintage Books, London, 2013, p. 40. In the United States, and elsewhere, the '46' component (weeks in the year) is nearer 48 or 50. And the 40 years is stretching to 45 and beyond.

7 Josephine Moulds, 'More Men Working Part-time Shows a Shift in Lifestyle Choice', *The Guardian*, 14 August 2014, https://www.theguardian.com/sustainable-business/men-part-time-work-lifestyle. I recently attended Timewise's impressive annual celebration of 'Power and Part-timers'. Of the 50 awards handed out, 43 were for women, and seven for men.

8 Marian Baird, Sara Charlesworth & Alex Heron, 'Flexible and Part-time Work in Australia: some responses to the need for work–life balance', Flexible_and_Part-time_work_in_Australia.pdf

9 'Final Remarks', in Tito Boeri et al. (eds.), *Women at Work: an economic perspective*, Oxford University Press, Oxford, 2005. *The Incomplete Revolution* is the title of Esping-Andersen's important book (Polity Press, Cambridge, 2009), in which he points out that the advances made so far by women generally have had some unintended consequences. These include the paradoxical one of widening the gap between households where both adults have higher qualifications and those where neither does — a major divide in many countries today. Assortative mating accentuates inequalities.

10 Interestingly, stepped retirement — going from full-time to declining weekly hours and eventually out from employment altogether — is something that men can quite easily accept, since they know that their

working lives do come to an end. Women, by contrast, may be 'stepping up' just as their partners are stepping down — a sign of their more complex life courses.

11 This line of argument has long historical roots. Carole Pateman identified what she calls the Wollstonecraft dilemma, after the radical 19th-century reformer. Mary Wollstonecraft argued that, as women have specific capacities, talents, needs, and concerns, so the expression of their citizenship will be differentiated from that of men. The problem is that this seems irreconcilable with a world in which paid work dominates, and is the key to citizenship. Pateman characterises the Wollstonecraft dilemma thus: 'The patriarchal understanding of citizenship means that the two demands are incompatible because it allows two alternatives only: either women become (like) men, and so full citizens; or they continue at women's work, which is of no value for citizenship.' Carole Pateman, *The Disorder of Women: democracy, feminism, and political theory*, Polity Press, Cambridge, 1990, p. 197.

12 The learned capacity to adapt to these changes has other, beneficial, consequences. When Michael Young and I studied how men and women adapted to leaving full-time employment at the end of their working lives, we found that many of the men were lost in a world where the job was no longer there to structure their daily lives. The women, by contrast, all had experience of changes of status, including spells out of employment looking after children (the study was done in the 1980s, and was thus of people whose adult lives had run from the mid-1950s), and so they had far greater capacity to manage the transition. Michael Young and Tom Schuller, *Life After Work*, HarperCollins, New York, 1990.

13 Jackie Ashley, 'Older Women: the nation's great untapped resource,' *The Guardian*, 10 December 2012, https://www.theguardian.com/commentisfree/2012/dec/09/older-women-great-untapped-resource. Data from the British Social Attitudes survey.

14 The British Social Attitudes survey reports that, since 1983, there has been a high level of concern about income inequality. In 2010, three-quarters of the public agreed that the income gap was too large. By 2012, this figure had risen to more than eight in ten.

15   See the 2016 Bib Gavron Memorial Lecture by Simon Walker: http://
     highpaycentre.org/pubs/text-of-simon-walker-bob-gavron-memorial-
     lecture-28.11.2016

16   'Widespread increases in income inequality have raised concerns about
     their potential impact on our societies and economies. New OECD
     research shows that when income inequality rises, economic growth
     falls. One reason is that poorer members of society are less able to
     invest in their education. Tackling inequality can make our societies
     fairer and our economies stronger.' Directorate for Employment,
     Labour, and Social Affairs, 'Focus on Inequality and Growth', OECD,
     December 2014, https://www.oecd.org/social/Focus-Inequality-and-
     Growth-2014.pdf

17   See http://highpaycentre.org/pubs/top-to-bottom-new-high-pay-centre-
     report-outlines-the-potential-for-wealth

18   For further argument, see Dalia Ben-Galim, 'Making the Case for
     Universal Childcare', Institute for Public Policy Research, 2011; Vidhya
     Alakeson and Alex Hurrell, 'Counting the Costs of Childcare', op. cit.;
     and Anne-Marie Slaughter, *Unfinished Business*, op. cit.

19   See http://www.particple.net/projects/view/5/101

20   Melissa Benn, *What Should We Tell Our Daughters?: the pleasures and
     pressures of growing up female*, John Murray, London, 2013.

21   See Iris Bohnet, *What Works*, op. cit. for many examples of how
     information and training needs to be combined with experiential
     methods to have any effect.

22   As the Parliamentary Select Committee on Women and Equality
     reported in 2016 on the idea of 'mid-life reviews': 'Over 3,000
     adults took part in reviews across England during the pilot period
     in 2013–2014 ... The mid-life career review has real potential for
     helping older women workers reconsider their options and broaden
     their horizons.' The UK Commission for Employment and Skills,
     'Making the Most of Women's Skills', Parliamentary Select Committee
     on Women and Equality, 2015, p. 59.

23   See Million Women Mentors, http://www.millionwomenmentors.org

24   For further argument, see Chartered Management Institute, http://
     www.managers.org.uk/paygap2

25 Tom Schuller and David Watson, *Learning Through Life: inquiry into the future for lifelong learning*, National Institute of Adult Continuing Education, 2009, http://www.learningandwork.org.uk/lifelonglearninginquiry/docs/IFLL-summary-english.pdf and 'Learning Through Life', 2009, www.niace.org.uk/lifelonglearninginquiry. See also Lynda Gratton and Andrew Scott, *The 100-Year Life: living and working in an age of longevity*, Bloomsbury, London, 2016.

26 See '3rd Global Report on Adult Learning and Education', op. cit.

27 Barry Golding et al. (eds.), *Men Learning Through Life*, National Institute for Adult and Continuing Education, Leicester, 2014.

28 See Tom Schuller and David Watson, *Learning Through Life*, op. cit., pp. 138–40.

29 See Linda Babcock and Sara Laschever, *Women Don't Ask*, op. cit. and Iris Bohnet, *What Works*, op. cit.

30 David Riesman et al. (eds), *The Lonely Crowd: a study of the changing American character*, Yale University Press, New Haven, 2001 (first published 1950).

31 Anne-Marie Slaughter, 'Why Women Still Can't Have It All', *The Atlantic*, July 2012, http://www.theatlantic.com/magazine/archive/2012/07/why-women-still-cant-have-it-all/309020. 'Default Man' is also the phrase used by the transvestite artist Grayson Perry in his critique of the current power establishment; see Grayson Perry, *The Descent of Man*, Penguin Books, London, 2016.

32 See Anna Coote and Jane Franklin (eds), *Time On Our Side: why we all need a shorter working week*, New Economics Foundation, London, 2013; and Martin Ford, *The Rise of the Robots*, Oneworld, London, 2016.

33 Lynda Gratton and Andrew Scott, *The 100-Year Life*, op. cit.

34 In due course, the introduction of the right to request flexible working time might come to be seen as a truly significant step forward in the United Kingdom, as it has been in the Netherlands. It does not force the employer to grant the request, but it builds awareness of a wider range of work-time options.

35 'Mental Capital and Well-being: making the most of ourselves in the 21st century', Foresight Mental Capital and Wellbeing Project, Government Office for Science, 2008, http://www.bis.gov.uk/foresight/our-work/

projects/published-projects/mental-capital-and-wellbeing/reports-and-publications. The gains suggested for an extension of flexible working to all adults were of the order of £250 million annually, though the report properly notes how difficult it is to produce a reliable precise figure.

36 House of Commons Select Committee on Women and Equality, 'Gender Pay Gap: second report of session 2015–16', op. cit., p. 83.

37 See http://www.timewisejobs.co.uk and http://www.sliversoftime.com. Some Australian workplaces are moving in this direction, but there are significant barriers to overcome; see Alex Heron et. al, 'Flexible and Part-time Work in Australia', op. cit.

38 See Juliet Schor, 'The Triple Dividend', in Anna Coote and Jane Franklin (eds.), *Time On Our Side*, op. cit., pp. 3–20.

39 This has recently become a major issue with the growth of the so-called 'gig economy', and debate over the status of those who work for firms such as Uber and Deliveroo. A recent (October 2016) UK employment tribunal judged that they should be regarded as employees entitled to holiday pay and other rights, rather than as self-employed.

40 The administrative costs alone are enormous: to administer a single claim for Income Support costs £181, and for Jobseekers Allowance, £82. See Malcolm Torry, *Money for Everyone: why we need a citizen's income*, Policy Press, Bristol, 2013, p. 87.

41 For a powerful and PP-relevant example of the perversities and injustices of the current tax/benefit set-up, see a recent report from session of the parliamentary national audit committee: 'Not counting the enormous pension tax reliefs or personal tax allowances, the treasury hands out £100bn a year in tax reliefs that are an accretion of past chancellors' whims and pet projects, full of nonsensical anomalies. She [Margaret Hodge, chair of the Committee] cites a small one: cleaners, nurses and other night shift workers can't claim against tax for their taxi fares to get home safely at night, but a lawyer, accountant or professional can.' Polly Toynbee, 'This Farcical Tax System is Cheating Us Out of Billions', *The Guardian*, 29 July 2014, http://www.theguardian.com/commentisfree/2014/jul/29/farcical-tax-system-cheating-billions-chase-avoiders

42 See Malcolm Torry, *Money for Everyone*, op. cit., for an exhaustive

account, or Citizens Income, http://www.citizensincome.org, for a rather more manageable one.

43 Martin Ford, *The Rise of the Robots*, op. cit., esp. Ch. 10.

44 Since I first drafted this section, there have been a number of major and quite hard-headed analyses that take the CI idea seriously, notably 'Creative Citizen, Creative State: the principle and pragmatic case for a Universal Basic Income', Royal Society for the Arts, 2015, http://www. thersa.org/discover/publications-and-articles/reports/basic-income, and Howard Reed and Stewart Lansley, 'Universal Basic Income: an idea whose time has come?', Compass, 2016, http://www.compassonline. org.uk/publications/universal-basic-income-an-idea-whose-time-has-come. Nationally, Switzerland held a national referendum on whether to introduce a basic income; it was decisively rejected, in part because the level was set unrealistically high. The Netherlands is introducing a basic income in several municipalities on a trial basis, and Finland is actively considering experimentation.

45 See Joseph Stiglitz et al., 'Report of the Commission on the Measurement of Economic Performance and Social Progress', op. cit. See also Anna Coote (ed.), *A New Economics of Time*, op. cit., and recent official moves to promote the measurement of wellbeing alongside conventional indicators of progress: 'ONS is developing new measures of national wellbeing. The aim is to provide a fuller picture of how society is doing by supplementing existing economic, social and environmental measures.' 'Measuring National Wellbeing', *The National Archives*, http://www.ons. gov.uk/ons/guide-method/user-guidance/well-being/index.html

46 See a recent YouGov poll in which 87% of British people, across all social and geographical boundaries, picked happiness as their society's goal, compared with 8% voting for money. The poll was conducted for Action for Happiness, and so needs to be treated with some caution, but is nevertheless indicative. See 'National Happiness Matters More Than National Wealth', *Action for Happiness*, 19 March 2014, http://www. actionforhappiness.org/news/national-happiness-matters-more-than-national-wealth

47 Lewis Mumford, *Technics and Civilization*, Harcourt, Brace & Company, San Diego, 1934, Ch. 8, Section 12.

Acknowledgements

My thanks go first to all the people who allowed themselves to be interviewed for this book. They have mostly been anonymised in the text, so I can't sensibly name them here. They were all generous with their time, and patient. Thanks also to those who helped me in arranging the interviews, especially Tom Wilson, Mary Alys (now sadly deceased), Pat Hurley, Frances Hunter, Jane Warwick, and Judith Chivers.

The book has benefitted greatly from comments at various stages. I had very constructive comments on the full text from friends — Sue Fyvel, Ann Gladstone, Peter Harris, Rosemary Milne — and from my daughter Bernie Coote. Satya Brink, Jay Ginn, and Anna Coote commented helpfully on particular chapters. Denise Winn made important editorial suggestions on overall style.

Several people helped with suggestions for Paula-relevant examples in fiction: Susan Avery, Ann Edmunds, Kathy Graham-Harrison, and Alfie Spencer. I am also grateful to Jenny Neugarten and Heather Joshi for their help with longitudinal information.

I have enjoyed the collaboration with Clo'e Floirat across the Channel. Her drawings complement the text very well, and give the book a closer resemblance to *The Peter Principle* (which used old *Punch* drawings).

Greg Donaldson has greatly helped by designing and supporting the website www.paulaprinciple.com.

My publisher, Scribe, has been been excellent to work with throughout. I'm particularly grateful to my editor, Julia Carlomagno, who suggested many improvements to the text.

Very welcome encouragement came, over the rather extended gestation period, from many people, especially Fay Lomax Cook and Bob Scott. My brother Andrew has been a most tenacious agent, going way beyond the call of fraternal duty. Finally, Prunella Gee has read and commented on the text, more than once, with unmatcheable attention to detail. I have involved her in rather too many Paula conversations, but her encouragement has never ever flagged, for which I am truly grateful.